BARTER

BARTER

How to get almost anything without money

CONSTANCE STAPLETON &
PHYLLIS C. RICHMAN

Charles Scribner's Sons

NEW YORK

Library of Congress Cataloging in Publication Data

Stapleton, Constance ——
    Barter.

        1. Barter. I. Richman, Phyllis C.,
joint author. II. Title.
HG230.7.R5   381   77-21624
ISBN 0-684-15193-6
ISBN 0-684-15283-5 (paper)

1 3 5 7 9 11 13 15 17 19   V/C   20 18 16 14 12 10 8 6 4 2
   3 5 7 9 11 13 15 17 19   V/P   20 18 16 14 12 10 8 6 4 2

Printed in the United States of America

CONTENTS

"All government, indeed every human benefit and enjoyment, every virtue, and every prudent act, is founded on compromise and barter."—EDMUND BURKE

WARNING:

The practice of barter can be habit-forming, resulting in permanent addiction.

This book is for informational purposes only and is not intended to be used as a course of instruction, nor is it an endorsement of some of the practices described within.

Only the reader can decide from personal experience or expert advice which barter transactions are taxable and which are governed by a higher rule: Golden, fair exchange, or, as they say in the trade, passing it on.

In all phases of barter, let the laws of the land be your guide and act accordingly.

INTRODUCTION

"What it is, if I raise something and you make something can't we make a trade? We could send 'em [other nations] all the politicians they need. For instance, Russia some Senators for some vodka. Little Nicaragua some Congressmen for some bananas. I tell you, the whole fool scheme is worth trying, just for the sake of this last part. If you can furnish the world with our politicians we can compete with 'em."

—WILL ROGERS

If you think barter came in with the Indians and died during the Depression, think again.

Although Nicaragua hasn't volunteered to send bananas for Congressmen yet, barter is alive and well, flourishing at every level of private and commercial life from trading comic books on the corner to securing billion-dollar rights behind boardroom doors.

That's quite a span to cover in a single book, so we won't. This is a primer of barter: for those who have never tried it; for those who are interested in perfecting their skills; as well as for those who want to know what's going on so that they don't get caught in a squeeze play and find themselves the bartered ones. (More complicated plays and maneuvers of advanced barter from international trade to scientific stakes will be explored in a later book.)

In its simplest terms, barter is a game in which each player trades what he doesn't need to get what he wants . . . and both players win. How you use barter depends on where you've been, what your needs are, and where you want to go. It's easy to play once you begin, and nine times out of ten it is the least expensive way to get from where you are to where you want to be. Practice will double the flavor, triple the value, and increase your standard of living many times over.

Once you get out of the habit of reaching for your wallet, checkbook, or credit card, you will discover that anything can be traded (time, goods, service, words, even influence) to get whatever you need. True, it takes a certain amount of time, imagination, and talent, but where else can you get a free education in values, human nature, salesmanship; reduce deficits; and clean out your closets—all at the same time? If you have tried carpooling or traded babysitting, you know how and have already begun. Try rearranging your thinking by substituting terms. Replace *money* in your thinking with *barter*. *Throwaways* will automatically become *get-to's; selling and buying* are converted to *trading;* and before you can say, "Barter," *price* will reappear as *value*.

Barter is not new. God first opened the game in the Garden of Eden by offering Adam a companion in exchange for one of his ribs, following that with free rent in return for not touching the fruit of one tree.

Today, barter can be used, among other things, to:

- *live on when money disappears (as after a holocaust, during food shortages, or when you've been fired)*
- *obtain rare, one-of-a-kind items unobtainable on the market*
- *get scarce commodities (as the government trades grain for minerals and metals)*
- *win legal settlements*
- *gain control of a situation*
- *take over a business*
- *improve credit*
- *unload chores you don't like*
- *decrease capital gains*
- *reduce taxes*
- *use what you learn to effect other barters*

· *trade assets and talents to gain experience*
· *earn a college education*
· *win a better job*
· *rearrange or redistribute assets*
· *enrich your life by sharing with others.*

Barter is the least theoretical yet the most specific of trading practices, enabling people without money to get anything they need without *owing* money. In primitive societies bartering is often the only game in town, with bartered items used, worn, or eaten; traded for other things; or kept to exchange for future needs. In different civilizations and geographical areas, the objects bartered can be material things such as shells, mats, baskets, cloth, tea, gold dust, skins, or dog teeth; or immaterial things such as songs, dances, planting, or even sorcery techniques. A frequently used item often becomes an official standard of exchange, with everything measured by comparison (if a knife costs 10 coconuts, a wife, depending on her beauty, family, or assets, may set you back 2,000 coconuts).

Since conditions and needs also affect barter, what is valuable one day can lose value the next (for example, if yams are currency, a good harvest would deflate the market). Captain Cook, discoverer of Hawaii, found that the increased supply of red feathers had lowered their value as a medium of exchange. As a consequence, currency with more than one use became more valuable: shells and metal disks could be worn, food eaten, and spears and hoes taken in trade used as tools and weapons (not at all unlike today's governments who trade weapons for military bases and wheat for oil).

Over the years the ceremonial exchanges of barter grew into permanent partnerships linking communities to each other in needs and practice. However, some chiefs used their positions of influence to create barter monopolies. A good chief might use his power to produce objects of wealth, canoes, large storehouses, and dwellings for his tribe, while others accumulated barter to wage war, pay a sorcerer to kill a man by witchcraft, or hire a man to spear an offender. Most tribes, however, used barter to keep food on the table and brides in the family, to preserve the status quo, to keep native industries going, and, through interdependence, to maintain peace.

When specific items such as metal crosses and sacred animals were used for barter with God for blessings received, anticipated, or requested, or to conciliate Him for past misdeeds, they then achieved religious significance. In Scandinavian mythology one's position in Valhalla depended on the amount of gold taken along, and other civilizations buried their dead with grain and canoes.

Interesting word associations also developed. Roman soldiers were paid in salt, with the phrase "not worth his salt" referring to the practice of trading slaves for their weight in salt. The word *wampum* used by American Indians was the Anglicized version of the Algonkian word meaning "string of white shells," and nearly every word in the Chinese language dealing with wealth is a sign for shell.

Everyone has heard how Manhattan Island was obtained for beads, but did you know that William Penn was granted 40,000 square miles (now known as Pennsylvania) in a political barter? Charles II owed Penn's father from $11,000 to $16,000 in loans, wages, and promised gifts. When the elder Penn died, leaving everything to his son, a Quaker (then politically unpopular as religion), the king was in an embarrassing position that he quickly erased by a barter. In payment of the debt, the king gave Penn the land, asking for only 20 percent of all gold and silver found there, plus an annual rent of two beaverskins, payable the first day of each January thereafter.

Early American textbooks often contained a chapter on barter, and when Harvard was young, student term bills could be paid in produce and livestock. In the first fifty to seventy years of our country, circulating currencies were unbelievably scanty; and because so many Americans printed their own money (including Benjamin Franklin), it depreciated fast in value and was almost always questionable. Whatever paper currency was available was viewed with distrust and used to pay taxes and attorneys' fees. If Americans did not barter, they often had to do without. The low value Americans placed on money is reflected in the 1810 census which showed the average income to be only $2 per capita.

Tobacco was a preferred currency worldwide for everything from slaves to brides. In 1620 and 1621 the Virginia Company imported 150 "young and uncorrupt girls" as wives for settlers who paid 100 pounds of tobacco for each wife, the price rising to 150 pounds as the demand rose. A shipping triangle from New England to Africa, across to the West Indies, and north to the Carolinas, Virginia, and Maryland formed the backbone of commerce; slaves and gold dust were traded for molasses and sugar, which was in turn made into rum (to be bartered for slaves and gold). Mills accepted a percentage of grain or wood processed in payment of bills; undertakers were paid wood for funeral bills; and farmers traded use of land for a percentage of the crop.

If you were in the right place at the right time, you could make a fortune. Gold miners reaching Utah during the '49 Gold Rush discovered (like many vacationers since) that they had packed the wrong things, and in order to lighten their load and travel faster, to get to the gold before someone else did, they traded off oxen, wagons, and provisions to Mormons for fast horses and fresh food. Quantity presented other problems in the barter network. When Henry Stanley set out to find David Livingstone in Africa in 1871, he tossed and turned at night wondering if the 60 tons of cloth and beads carried by his 200-man safari would be enough to do the job.

Until the late 1930s, stores like Quynn's Hardware in Frederick, Maryland, carried a large volume of barter on their books as "bill in bar," including teaching, pasture rent, eggs, and bearskins. In fact, one reason so many pieces of rare Amelung glass can be found in the Frederick area is that Mr. Amelung paid his bill in glass, which was then traded for other things.

Thomas Edison proposed a U.S. experiment with a commodity dollar of constant purchasing power backed by goods (in 1922), but unlike his electric light, it never caught on. Once Americans started using money they became great innovators. Easily divided and stored, simple to recognize, money did not rot, could be carried in one's pocket, and was certainly faster to process than cows. It became the favored medium of exchange until the 1930 Depression, which turned people once again to self-help and barter.

During World War II barter tapered off in the United States as jobs and money became plentiful, but it was used by Nazi Germany to gain business in world markets. Refugees fleeing Europe converted assets into gems which could be easily transported and later converted into any country's currency, and American GIs found that bartering chocolate, stockings, coffee, tobacco, and sugar brought richer rewards than money. In China cigarettes were worth more than Chinese money, and after the war in Germany a cigarette was the best tip in a restaurant, with a Leica camera costing only two packs.

Once you realize that international trade started by bartering brides, you recognize that even the most political barter may have personal undertones. It took Columbus six years of negotiating with Queen Isabella for ships to sail to America because her wise men kept telling her he was asking for too large a percentage of the bounty. Today, governments barter for power, trade, or simply to get the job done. Seats on committees, equal time on TV, trading rights, dams, power plants, peace treaties, trading POWs and spies, political kidnappings, nuclear blackmail, and influence-peddling are all forms of barter—some out in the open, others under the table.

Small towns barter taxes for maintenance, free parking to merchants in return for bonds to build parking decks. Larger communities trade assets for needed water. Cities barter for federal funds to build highways; promotion councils trade extras and discounts to attract companies and conventions. Members of state legislatures vote against funding for competitive areas until the other side agrees to give them something for their backyard. A Russian-born Greek citizen, George Costakis, recently bartered 80 percent of his art collection to the Soviet Union in return for the government's permission to let him take the remaining 20 percent out of the country and, as part of the deal, retain his Moscow apartment for future visits to Moscow.

American museums and National Parks often find themselves victims of elegant sufficiency in what they don't need because a collection happened to be in their neighborhood when the owner died, while objects they need to tell the region's history are somewhere else. Because they cannot sell such objects, Congress passed the Museum Act, enabling parks to exchange artifacts. Since then, the American public has been enriched in many ways.

Battlefields have been able to barter for period guns by trading artifacts in their possession which often turn out to be the exact pieces needed to complete another museum's puzzle. The National Collection of Fine Arts now contains a Thomas Moran painting obtained for two paintings of *The Buffalo Hunt* by a lesser artist, which the National Park Service needed to tell the story of a western park. Because most of the original chairs used by the First Federal Congress in the Senate Chamber of Congress Hall at Independence Historic National Park in Philadelphia were worn out or had disappeared over the years, reproductions were made; but in recent years, a few of the originals have been traded back for the reproductions by owners who wanted the American people to have the real thing.

In science, brainpower is the basic coin of exchange. How and what a scientist barters is often in direct proportion to how much money is at his disposal. For instance, if he is working on a low budget, he barters for additional space, workers, animals, reagents, equipment, a better job, or trips and expenses necessary to enhance his research. When he is engaged in a project for which money is plentiful, barter can be used to cut through administrative red tape or gain valuable collaboration on papers and experiments, more and better assistance, a wider circle of influence, cooperation from other institutions, consultation, writing, or even recognition.

In recent years, because of the heightened interest and action in barter, the IRS has started to examine transactions with an eye to collecting its share of the action. Although no money is exchanged, the trading of services or goods represents income and must therefore be reported as income and taxed. Taxes are determined by market value whether or not you pay market price, but only on the profit. After you subtract your original cost, repairs, and so on, there may not be a profit to be taxed.

Some barters are deductible as business expense (see Professionals and Taxes); realtors trade off "in kind" properties to obtain maximum depreciation (see Land); and the IRS tends to overlook barters between neighbors, friends, and relatives, as well as small and informational barters. However, they are concerned with company or business barters that appear to be engineered for tax purposes. What matters is intent. If the IRS discovers that something was made to appear as a gift or a loss when it actually is a barter, it will be displeased. What is great in theory sometimes does not work out in practice. While it would appear that the IRS has not decided certain barter issues, if there is the slightest doubt in your mind, consult your tax adviser before you become a test case (see Taxes for further specifics).

Self-help, or exchange of goods, labor, services, skills, surpluses, treasures, information, or influence, can be used to obtain anything you want, anytime, anywhere, with anyone. Everybody has something somebody else wants, and few can resist the attraction of "something for nothing."

Although the stakes are often vastly different, the rules are always the same. Timeless, self-balancing, thriving on repetition and goodwill, barter's imperfections are reducible while its opportunities are limitless. Valuable in good times for improving the quality of life, barter is survival's tool, reappearing in more ingenious dress each time inflation drives down the value of money.

Have you ever tried going without money, checks, or credit cards? Do you think you could? How long do you think you'd last? Three months? Three days? Three minutes?

It's hard to stop once you start. Before you know it, addiction sets in. The game builds momentum. You begin to see and explore more opportunities, multiplying skills and contacts as you go. Before long, you're specializing in what you do best; your barters leap in value, as much as five times over, reducing your investment in labor or time, leaving more time for more barters.

As word spreads, kindred spirits who want to make deals will find their way to your door. Your children will be bartering their way through college. You'll be gaining services without bills, assets without money, while experiencing a rebirth of independence.

You'll discover, as barterers have since time began, that dealing on a one-to-one basis is fun, because sharing and caring grow in ways money never can. In recognizing and dealing with value systems of partners, you develop a deeper understanding of your own. Like Midas, who received his golden touch in return for a kindness, you realize that you are not losing time or goods, but sharing life.

Join the movement. Reuse, recycle, regenerate.

Down with cash! Up with barter!

BARTER

Getting Started

"If a man has good corn, or wood, or boards, or pigs to sell or can make better chairs or knives, crucibles or church organs than anybody else, you will find a broad, hardbeaten path to his house, though it be in the woods."

—Ralph Waldo Emerson

Everyone has something that someone else wants. At jamborees Boy Scouts swap patches. As skills develop, they trade stamps, berets, equipment, and after returning home, letters and visits.

When you start depends to a large extent on your needs. One of us discovered hers at an early age, living next to a candy store that did a land office business in penny candy. There was only one hitch: she didn't have a penny. But she did have an empty garage. In a desperate effort to snare her share of the penny market, she spent days building a haunted house destined to lure every kid off West Street.

It didn't work. Nobody came. After a day of agonizing over why her haunted house extravaganza didn't sell, she sat down on the curb to do an analysis of the neighborhood. What could she put in her showcase that would attract those pennies? The answer appeared in the person of her brother, a curly-headed rogue who wasn't above sitting in the back of the garage in return for half the take. The merchandising message of the sign was to the point and sold the product. "Kisses, 2¢," it advertised. The two of them took in a month's worth of pennies and got sick spending the profits.

The formula worked so well that she used it to take over her brother's gang. For months she had been scheming to get into the group, but all her efforts reaped was rejection. Her recent garage sale proved she had aimed too low. Why not, she decided, take over the gang? She convinced them she could design a hideout in the woods requiring absolutely no money, one that would be the envy of Tarzan and every other gang in town. They bought the deal and started working for her the next day, building a fern hut that smelled better than Tarzan and was a lot more fun than all his monkeys.

Some people don't discover a need until they get older. When twenty-two-year-old college junior Paul Ferbank discovered that spouses of professors didn't have to pay tuition at Hobart College in Geneva, New York, he knew immediately how he could save $3,400 annually and pass on a tax savings to someone else. His ad in the local newspaper started: "Needy tax-deductible male student seeking marriage contract for tuition purposes."

Most people don't have to be talked into bartering if they have tried it before. In fact, they are often waiting for someone else to bring it up. When you do, they will light up, grin all over, and hug you in disbelief. If you run into someone who has never tried it before, teach him or her how. You'll get a plus on your side of the ledger and probably find a lifetime friend.

All realization is a direct result of expectation. If you expect rejection for your efforts, that's exactly what you will get. If you realize you are doing people a favor and helping them save money, you'll end up with more barter partners than you can handle.

Where do you find them? Anywhere and everywhere. Among family members, in the neighborhood, through newspaper ads and notices on church bulletin boards, at the local Elks hall. Just remember: if it moves, it can barter. If it doesn't move, it can *be* bartered.

When you first begin, practice in local leagues with those at the same stage of development so that you aren't overcome by the competition. When opportunity knocks, don't be nervous. Speak up. You have nothing to lose and everything to gain. In all probability, the other person wants a trade as much as you do. If he doesn't, check out Rules of the Game for ways to tip the scales in your favor.

The following chapter tells you how to discover talents you didn't know you had, as well as how to channel them. After that, Rules of the Game explores methods of procedure and shows you how to invent a few of your own. The middle part of the book delves into all kinds of barter, in alphabetical order for easy reference or for skimming. You can check out those that interest you or read them all, concluding with spinoffs, side effects, and branching out.

If you find offers sometimes catch you unaware or ill prepared, keep a mental list of barterables; or each time you come across something you can do without, jot it down. Keeping track of barterables is as easy as keeping a grocery list.

Then, the next time you want or need anything, instead of reaching for your checkbook or wallet . . . stop. Put on your biggest grin. Look the other guy dead in the eye and say, "I love it. Now, what would you take in barter?"

Believe us, it's better.

Finding Out What You Have to Trade

"Never start a vast project in a half vast way."

—ANONYMOUS

Come on, be honest. That's the only way you can separate what you want from what you need; because the two may not necessarily be the same.

Do you have more time or more talent? Talent is worth twice as much in a trade, but the more time you have to barter, the faster you can build up your skills and talents to make your time count double.

If you don't know what you can do, make a list of everything in which you have taken secret delight: the essay prize in high school, setting up a "fun house" in the garage when you were young, playing hooky, redecorating your room for 25 cents on the installment plan, getting along with your mother-in-law. No matter how insignificant it seems, write it down.

Then make a list of everything you secretly hate, anything that makes your teeth itch: women's clubs, golf, housekeeping, long hair, martinis. Again, don't hold back. This is your life you're improving! The secret is to fill up your life with more of the things you like and to dispose, through barter, of those you hate.

Next, make a list of everything you think you do well. It doesn't matter how far-fetched it is; put it down. Balancing the checkbook, canning, freezing, driving, writing, pet tending, reading, organizing jobs or space. Somewhere out there is someone who needs you.

Now comes the crunch. List those habits and personality traits for which you are most criticized: talking too much on the phone, having your nose stuck in a book all the time. All of your excesses, whether time, space, things, or habits, can be traded. If you have a critical temperament, apply to the local paper to become a food or theater critic in return for free passes. Read too much? Trade reading aloud to someone with poor vision. Be a tutor. If you are a telephone hog, volunteer as telephone chairman for a local organization or club in return for a free membership.

Did you know that every vice is an exaggeration of a virtue? It's true. List everything that is wrong with your location and see how you can work it over to the credit side of the ledger. For instance, you live in the country. It's too far to commute to the city. That's the disadvantage. How can you turn it into an advantage? Take in guests on weekends in return for help with the gardening. Trade an upstairs room to a writer for a weekend of writing in return for free stay-overs at his pad in the city.

You never need to throw anything away. Your leftovers are somebody else's feast. Outdated clothes are valuable costumes or materials for hooking rugs. Nor should your possessions grow to feel neglected through underuse. You can hardly use your lawnmower more than once a week, but the money-hungry kid down the block can, taking care of your yard in exchange. Your thirty-cup coffee pot could be serving your neighbor's party while you enjoy his newest books. Somebody needs your office space while you are on vacation, not to mention your house and your watchdog.

Set goals even if you hate the word. Doing so gives direction to your efforts. Try filling up a page with everything you want out of life. Then select the three most important goals and the steps necessary to reach them. (You may be surprised at what you leave off the list—it's a real eye-opener.) Then ask yourself, if money were no object for the next six months, how you would change your life. Travel? Better clothes? You may discover you don't want that much change and that you can easily rearrange what you are now doing to make your dream come true. And last but not least, if you had three months to live, how would you change your current lifestyle? If your first list surprised you, this last may shock you. What it does is to separate your wants from your needs, your thirst for money from your need to improve the quality of life. Ideally it will pin down your needs, help you to look at your life objectively and discard all the unnecessaries.

Now it's time to find your barter half.

Rules of the Game

Rules are made to be broken; that's the first rule. Like learning primary colors in art, if you know what combinations are available and test them, you will soon be devising your own variations.

The opening section discussed what barter is, why you should play, what you can expect to gain, how to analyze your assets and focus play while developing scope. If you haven't learned it yet, there's one rule always to remember: anything can be bartered; anyone can play; everyone can win. (Some just take more time than others.) It is now time to take stock of what pieces you can mentally or physically stack on your side of the board; how to find other players and interest them in accepting the challenge; when to open; rules of play; tactics, techniques, negotiations, follow-through, contracts needed along the way, and, when necessary, legal action.

Throughout this book you will discover additional things to trade that you never thought could be traded. We've already touched on a few, such as talent, time, space, goods, information, services, influence, employment, inheritance, ideas, skills, equipment, and family; but did you know that all of these factors can also be multiplied, subtracted, or divided? If the other party does not meet the terms you set, subtract part of your original offer, or change terms of ownership, allowing him just to co-own the object, or restrict its use to certain times of the day or year. Make substitutions if you feel his ante is not enough. Suggest only borrowing, and cut the ante back to a fraction. Until you come down to the contract, terms can be arranged and rearranged as many times as you like. If you can't agree, perhaps this isn't the right trading partner for you, and Mr. Right will soon be coming around the bend. If there is something you want very much but you can't come up with enough ideas or barterables to get it, find partners willing to co-own it with you. A racehorse, for instance, often has as many as ten owners. When you hit the big time or the more expensive spreads such as land, sharing may be the only way to get your foot in the door.

How do you multiply? Easy. In figuring value, talents and skills are worth twice as much as straight time. On the other hand, if a person's greatest lack is time and you know it, and there is no competition, you may be able to swing a one-for-one deal (but don't count on it). Once you become highly specialized, or even get a corner on the market so that there is no other source for what you have or can do, your value may skyrocket to ten times as much, and if what you have cannot be obtained anywhere in the world, up to one hundred times. Each case depends on the persons involved, the needs or limitations to be met, and any time frame.

In barters between lawyers and plumbers, for instance, it should be decided whether the job basis is one-for-one or hour-for-hour, or whether each will charge his hourly rate and then will swap bills afterward.

There is also the negative barter, used to build up leverage on your side. By increasing the competition (subtly letting the other person know), holding back on the terms, or adding pressure to the time element, you can effect a faster settlement or one more beneficial to you. If, on the other hand, the other party tries these tactics to force your hand, use poker tactics by not letting him know how much you want the trade. For instance, when a company on the rocks needs to be reorganized and redirected, the right person can name his own terms to do the job; but if he makes the first contact, his power may be diluted almost by half. If he finds the right middleman to tout his abilities to the company so that they make the first move, his power in bargaining is greater. Using the right skills in negotiating, he can demand rights of hiring and firing, stock, fringe benefits, and percentages and may even end up owning the company outright without spending a cent, by trading his management talents (see Big Business).

Initial contact (see Public Relations and Promotion) greatly affects power throughout the play. When the other person comes to you, it puts you in the driver's seat. Contacts and opportunities that come your way are in direct proportion to the number you make. The world will never beat a path to your door if it doesn't know where you live.

From the first contact until the deal is closed, there is one other factor that greatly influences every play, and that is the strength of your personality. If the other person likes you, he will be easier to deal with and more pleasant to follow through. Therefore, get to know him as well as possible before opening negotiations.

Where do you find trading partners? That depends on what you want to trade (see various chapters throughout the book for more information). One of the most effective methods, if you have the time, is to pass the word among your friends. In all probability, having the same taste in friends will produce the right goods or services in greater proportion. Advertising in general publications will bring many replies that have to be sifted and sorted. If you want to protect your privacy, use a box or telephone number. Don't give out your address until you are fairly sure a deal can be struck.

In advertising, say "For Sale or Trade"—it will bring more prospects. But set a value or price for your object first to make the dealing go more easily. The other party may not have traded before and may need all the help he can get.

Other places to look for prospects are company newsletters, specialized publications, fraternal organizations, bulletin boards in community halls and grocery stores, the library, the yellow pages of the telephone directory. It may take many phone calls in the beginning, but as you become more proficient and specialized, you will be able to cement a deal with a single call. In any case, it is wise to make sure you are dealing with the owner or person in charge. The best deal in the world is no deal at all if the barterer doesn't own the merchandise.

Bert Thornton, a skilled barterer in media and public relations and owner of WTRI in Brunswick, Maryland, learned this lesson the hard way while in high school. Freshmen weren't allowed to attend the senior prom, but he figured a way to get around the rules as well as to get in free. He offered to design and make the decorations for the upperclassmen in return for going to the prom. "It was green light all the way," Bert remembers, "right up to the big night when the principal said no." From that day on, Bert has made it a point to talk to the person in charge.

Sometimes the person who has what you want has never thought about unloading it. Put the idea into his head. If that isn't effective, work on his friends and family. Find out what his hobbies or consuming interests are and cater to them. If you don't have what he wants, find someone who does and get them together. It may break the log jam in his thinking. In fact, it may be so effective that *he* talks *you* into the trade. Bring up the subject at the right time. It's easier to talk a farmer into trading off unused machinery in the winter than at the height of harvest when he's faced with the possible need to replace equipment that breaks down. On the other hand, leave yourself enough time to make a deal so that you are not pushed for time or caught off balance. As Barbara Fritchie said, "Necessity never made a bargain."

Make sure all the pieces are in place before you make the first

move or open the play. Know the market. Establish the value of
what you have, as well as of what you want to get. This may involve comparison shopping in stores and newspapers and making
a few phone calls, but the more you know, the more strongly you
can deal when the action heats up, and the more sources you will
find for future barters if the first doesn't work out. Decide in advance exactly how far you will go to get what you want. If the price
is too high or the terms do not suit you, it may not be worth it. Too
much of what you already have is no bargain, nor is too high a
price, because you will never be able to trade it at a future date.
Get the most for what you have by seeking price information at the
right source; for instance, take a painting to an art specialist rather
than an antique dealer who may be appraising only the frame.

A well-known artist who barters for all his needs has several
ways of opening the negotiations. "I get to know a person by having him perform a service and owing him money. I usually ask
beforehand whether he will consider exchanging his services for
my work, but sometimes it occurs as an afterthought.

"In terms of determining equivalent value, I have run into problems but these are usually solved when the barteree sends a bill or
estimates the cost. Since my work has a going market value, I can
show him things of equivalent value. Many times, prospects end
up buying additional items over and above the amount being settled." The only person to say no to date was the septic tank man.
"After looking over the artwork, he shook his head and said, 'My
wife only collects plates,' so I wrote him a check."

It is also wise to establish whether the other person can obtain
what you have from another source. Bring it up in a casual way.
Lay the offer on the line, state the terms you think are adequate, or
put the offer two ways and let him choose which he likes better.
Start lower and work up to what you expect to pay; you may get it
for less than you expect. Don't act anxious or you will add ante
to the other side. Have a list of alternatives to take off some of
the pressure. For instance, in exploring values before you make the
offer, make a list of other parties who might be interested. If the
first deal doesn't come off, start canvassing the others. If you can't
find a match, come back to the first party and renegotiate. The in-
tervening time may have softened his position.

Save the best part of the barter to offer last, as the clincher. Indians always have a "holdback" or "deal finisher," which is the best and played last as a climaxer. It may be the straw that breaks the camel's back of resistance. How well you know the other person also has a great deal to do with the manner of play. If you can take time, when you meet resistance, try coming back with an easy interim barter, offering him something for much less than you know it's worth. He may find it irresistible, think you don't know much about value, and become easier to deal with in the future. This is a favorite ploy of antique dealers when they want to buy several items from a private seller.

The greatest bargains come out of season. Waiting until the need is greatest (for example, trading skis in the winter rather than the summer) will improve your position. You can also push for a better position if you know the other person is up against a deadline (he's leaving on a ski vacation the next day).

Throughout the bargaining don't be afraid to ask questions. You have nothing to lose and everything to gain. You may be giving him credit for knowing more than he does. If there is the slightest doubt in his mind, it will show up in evasion or misinformation. Once you find a weak spot, explore it. He may come down in terms. When he asks you questions, answer in as few words as possible. No sense giving him information he doesn't know—he may use it as leverage to weaken your position.

If he holds out for too high a price, find subtle ways to educate him. Reinspect the merchandise and find something wrong that he doesn't know exists. Ask a friend to go along and volunteer an outside opinion. Form another basis of comparison that will guarantee to make the item look inferior. Or find problems with the details, such as transportation. If it's something large, suggest that he deliver it to your house at a time you know will not be convenient for him. Then offer to pick it up yourself in return for better terms. Ask for maintenance for ninety days, if it has working parts. Or, if it's old, point out some of the problems of longevity.

If he is especially hard-nosed in the trading, do something that will throw him off balance. Drop your papers on the floor and let him help you pick them up. If he has been moving at a fast pace, slow down, and then when he appears to be losing patience, go faster than he does. Or start to stammer.

Even if he comes out with a flat no, don't give up. Try again. You may not have taken his sensitivities into consideration. Return to "Go" and analyze them. If his needs are related to status, feed him compliments. Sometimes needs are imaginary (I want to keep this thing because everyone in the neighborhood has one and as long as I live here I need it). On the other hand, his reservations may be very real. Maybe his mother gave it to him and it has sentimental value. Once you convince him that you treasure it as much as he does, you may get it for less—or nothing. Maybe all he needs is an ego massage. Introduce him to his idol, or if your name is worth something, endorse his favorite cause or invite him to your club.

Some barterers enjoy playing the game so much they are afraid to agree to terms because that means the game is over. If this is the case, suggest future plays so this one can be concluded. Other barterers don't like to play at all, which means you have to find other reasons for them to agree. Rearrange the merchandise in different quantities. Stretch the time factor, perhaps putting ownership on a trial basis. Rearrange terms, work on friends, or if what you have is very special, get the local newspaper to write an article about it to make the bait more alluring. If he still doesn't bite, offer part payment in cash. If the other person purchased it inexpensively, he may feel he can cover his investment while getting something else free.

Adapt your manner of play to the arena at hand. If conservative, play safe with style. If freewheeling, spin your wheels faster. If it looks like a bad deal, know when to quit. Shake hands and walk away. He may come after you.

If you run into none of the above problems, or solve them and arrive at a trade, make the terms as simple as possible. The more details involved, the greater the risk for error or misunderstanding. Make sure that the exact amounts of goods or hours are determined and that the time requirement if any (hours of labor and when), deadlines on work and delivery, guarantees, and limitations are set. Leave nothing to chance, especially if you do not know the other person. Determine who pays for materials. Sometimes the person desiring the service does so (carpentering); in other deals the person giving pays (dentist); while others split all costs down the middle, including transportation. Also set down terms for collecting in case of default. Once all the details are worked out, put it all in writing. If the other person doesn't follow through (because of intent, illness, or even death), remember that verbal agreements don't work in court. However, the simplest written agreement listing terms and signed by both parties is as good as cash if you need to collect at a later date. Try to end all bartering on a friendly note, even when negotiations fall through. The ideal barter is when each one thinks he got the better deal. If negotiations hit a snag or more time is involved as the barter progresses, stop and renegotiate. If the other person doesn't follow through, give him a phone call. If that doesn't work, stop by and see him and follow that with a strong letter. If all else fails take legal action.

As you increase your barters, you will occasionally receive offers of something you don't want or need and there are no other offers on the horizon. If you don't really need what you are trying to trade and the other person wants it, consider taking the unwanted item to barter for something else. (Of course, if it's a lot of something that has no value, don't bother.) You may be able to find an interested party and be the go-between or middleman for a percentage, or a favor to keep in your mental credit bank to cash in on in a future barter. With practice you will see possibilities that involve several parties, like parlays or multi-barters.

A multi is a barter in which you find something you want in the wrong place but know where something is that the owner may be interested in trading. Sometimes you have to bet on yourself and make the deal immediately; but at other times you can put holds on everything while you work out the details. A safecracker opened a safe for the local post office, but then the postmaster couldn't pay the $150 tab because the government was sending a new safe in a few months. A deal was arranged. The old safe would be left until the new one arrived, then given in payment of the bill. In the interim (leaving each thing in its place) the safecracker traded the safe for a Model A car, which he in turn traded to a collector for an almost new car which he gave to his son for a sixteenth-birthday present. With no money down and a few minutes' work on a multi-barter, he got a free car.

In a parlay, you start with one thing and by trading arrive where you want to be. Teen-ager Kurt Ziebell took on a litter of thirteen puppies to save them from going to the pound, but when he couldn't keep them, he sold them for $10 each, and with the $130 bought a horse and saddle, which he traded for a go-cart and $200; and then he swapped that for a motorbike, which he traded in on a car.

Other kinds of barters include one-to-ones (straight out between two people); the implied ("you owe me and I will collect at a future date"); and the triple play (three things in three different locations; the barter is arranged by one person and each picks up what he wants from the original owner). The open-ended is the best (you find a good barter half and never quit doing each other favors).

If you play fair, keep your sense of humor, are dependable on follow-through, and always try to see the other guy's point of view, your barters will get better with practice, and you will constantly find new ways of playing by the old rules. Remember that anything can be traded, anyone can play, and everyone wins. Bet on yourself. Never think small; it doesn't take any more time to dream big.

Then relax and enjoy the game. It's the best group therapy in town.

Antiques

One Man's Junk Is Another Man's Antique

Wheeling and dealing in antiques can teach you more ways to barter than you realized existed.

Because the supply of authentic antiques is limited and the number of people searching for them is on the increase, barter is often the only way to acquire rare pieces. As a result, collectors habitually buy extras to trade for those items they need. They also buy up anything available in their specialty so that they can corner the market and name their own price—which nine times out of ten is not money, but more of what they already have. Because one-of-a-kind items are priceless, they are essentially worth any price to a collector—which is one reason why prices at collectors' auctions go so high you wonder if the bidders are using real money or printed paper from Monopoly.

In antiques, knowledge is power. The more you have, the faster you can recognize what no one else sees, as well as know its value. In building up collections, there is a distinct ratio between time and money. The more time you have (to search for antiques, deal with sellers, stay at auctions), the less money you will have to spend. Time, experience, and knowledge are useful trading cards toward what you want.

If you know more than others about native antiques and early history, people will seek you out for advice and appraisals, giving you first choice of particularly desirable pieces before others know they are for sale. Knowing the practices of local auctions will also put you in a better position to wheel and deal. For instance, can you buy unadvertised items off the floor before the auction? Do auctioneers knock down items (sell fast at a low price) to favorite bidders or to speed up the auction? Can you talk them into keeping an antique in the regular auction rather than saving it for a catalog sale so that you can pick it up for a lower price? To gain in experience and influence, offer to help at auction (sorting merchandise, carrying and passing during the sale, clerking, and so on). Depending on the volume of sales, they may pay you by the hour, give you credit on your bill, or furnish you with the opportunity to examine items and learn about them, as well as learn who the top dealers are and how they bid. If you see dealers bidding on something you don't recognize, put it on your research list so that you will know more about it the next time.

Before long, you will not only know more about antiques, but about how to research them, giving you another valuable trading card. Figure out how much your time is worth, then offer to research antiques for dealers who don't have the time. Keep lists of their specialties. Ask them if they will pay you a finder's fee, give you a discount at their shops in return for finding items on their list, or allow you to trade tips (of prospective buyers and/or merchandise) for credit.

Find out what a dealer needs other than antiques, then see how you can use this need as barter. If he doesn't have time to go to auctions, offer to bid for him in return for credit at his shop or permission to put a purchase on his bill (agreeing ahead of time on price). This is easier to arrange than you might realize. Top dealers not only do not have the time to attend auctions but usually do not want to be seen bidding. Armed with a list of what he wants, a map layout showing where it is, and the top price he wishes to pay, you can go to the auction while he tends the shop. Keeping price lists for antiques publications and annual price guides is another way to make time at auctions pay off. You may receive only minimal pay, or subscriptions, but the practice will train your eye to recognize value.

Alternatively, you can offer to mind the shop while a dealer goes to auction or on vacation, taking your pay in credit or antiques. You will gain experience as a dealer, establish contacts, learn about prices, value, sources of supply, and will soon be getting discounts there and at other shops. The owner may also let you use his tax number, as his subcontractor, for your purchases.

Other ways to use time as credit for antiques: if you frequent antique lectures and forums, taking notes for your own information, why not make copies, offering them to dealer friends in return for information, a free appraisal, discount, or favor? If you are a skilled refinisher, offer your services to a dealer for merchandise or credit. An artist can suggest sales tags large enough to contain a description, or design calling cards, stationery, or a brochure. A writer? Create some ads or offer to write a mimeographed flyer, auction notice, or even an article about his shop for the local newspaper. Have you an extra room or building? Trade him storage for his surplus inventory in return for credit.

Or try your hand at "picking." Many dealers start in antiques as pickers (buying for other dealers), but if the term turns you off, call yourself a "wholesaler." Keep lists of what several dealers specialize in. If you know what you are doing, it is easy to pick up enough buys at auction, sell off what you don't need on the way home, and end up with enough profit to pay your bill. Another way to make auctions pay is to buy several lots for a single bid and sell off what you don't want to people in the crowd. If there are several auctions in a single day, begin early enough so that you can check them out before starting time, staying at the sale with the greatest bargains and leaving bids with the auctioneers at the rest. This is one of the best ways to make other people's time pay, because although the auctioneer will not go over your bid, you will often get an item for less than your reserve, whereas if you had stayed in the crowd, you might have had to bid higher than you wanted to pay.

You can almost always use antiques in place of money as down payment or full payment for other antiques, and nearly every dealer will let you trade in antiques that you bought at his shop for the original price toward another purchase (lowering the price as well as the tax). Antiques are always going up in value, are difficult to replace, and are worth at least as much as you paid for them originally.

Another way to save money and use your time as barter is to become a dealer. In addition to getting permanent discounts of 10 to 50 percent from other dealers, you will be eligible to barter whole inventories, which many dealers do on a regular basis to keep their merchandise moving. Just because you get a license doesn't mean you have to open a shop. Some collectors get a dealer's license to avoid paying sales tax, or to gain entry to wholesale antique dealers. If you specialize, you will also save time because the antiques will come to you. Some dealers are open only by appointment or sell only to the trade; others buy antiques by the houseful, keep what they want, and sell off what is left at auction on the premises. One Pennsylvania dealer who does this on a regular basis increases his money at least tenfold on each house. This money also allows him to outbid all competition at auction. Dealers can put signs in their windows: "We Will Barter," listing items wanted. If you know your specialty, you will make a profit on every trade.

Another advantage to holding a dealer's license (obtainable for only $1 in most states) is that you can form your own wholesale ring and enjoy the benefits of group purchasing. Top dealers realized long ago that their appearance at auction often boosted prices, and outbidding each other pushed the prices beyond everyone's reach. Now dealers form private syndicates, with one member bidding at auction and the group meeting a few days later at a private sale to bid among themselves for what they want.

If being a dealer doesn't appeal to you, there are other ways to use your time as money to acquire antiques. Help with the church bazaar to be in on the ground floor and get first choice of items. Serve time on a fund-raising or acquisition committee of the local historical society, museum, or restoration group. Many donated items not in keeping with the period of a building are traded for other items or sold at reduced prices through personal contacts to procure money, which can then be used to buy what is needed. Because such institutions don't want to broadcast the fact that a gift is not being kept in their permanent collection, you must be discreet about such transactions or you will not be called another time.

Dig at the dumps. They are not as plentiful as they once were but are lucrative sources for old bottles, furniture, and antique hardware. Try the local junkyard, too. Befriend the town wrecker. He has a local storehouse full of marvelous architectural details, tradeables, and hardware. Keep what you want, selling or trading the rest for a profit. Enter flea markets as a seller to get first choice of other people's merchandise. It's a great way to trade off your surplus for what you want.

Watch for things others may miss such as amusement parks or old stores going out of business. Offer to buy or trade services for items before they are sold in order to cut out competition and get a lower price. Scan newspaper articles and ads for news of schools and churches being renovated. Stained-glass windows, pews, bells, architectural details are often available for a nominal price, or free in return for the labor of removing them. Divorced and retired individuals often trade antiques in return for labor or services. If you know that the local plumber or electrician is an auction buff, ask if he will work in return for antiques. While you're at house auctions, check basements, attic eaves, and barns for items overlooked for the sale. Offer to pay the owner for what you want. Chances are you'll get what you find free. Be generous with your knowledge and offer assistance in pricing or appraising antiques. It will put you first in line to buy or trade at your own price.

Offer to clean out garages, basements, and attics in return for keeping or selling items you find. Realtors often must hire someone to clean out a property after the seller leaves, before the new owner moves in. You could also manage a garage sale, or price items in return for what you want.

Plan to travel or vacation in out-of-the-way places; watch for things others overlook, such as windmills no longer in use, unusual birdhouses, whirligigs. Recognize antiques that have been converted to other uses (for instance, beds made into garden seats). More often than not, they can be reconverted at little cost and great profit.

Whenever you use time, knowledge, or surplus to purchase antiques, your expertise will grow; and you will discover that like antiques, time and talent are worth more than money in the bank.

Autos: Repairs, Tires, and Gas

Drive a Hard Bargain

If you think you can't afford a car because you don't have enough money, rearrange your thinking and take stock of what you can trade. Free automobiles are easier to come by than you realize. If you don't believe us, check out the history book, starting with Henry Ford.

Henry, who gained a reputation for paying "cash on the barrelhead" in later years, was turned down repeatedly in the beginning by investors who considered his venture speculative. Despite this, he continued knocking on doors, pushing ahead on faith, hope, and nerve, using his invention as collateral until he found businessmen willing to invest their assets in return for some of the stock. In 1903 John and Horace Dodge, who had established a machine shop which Henry needed to produce his car, agreed to make the motor, transmission, and other parts and put up $7,000 in materials and their note for $3,000. In return, Henry gave each of them fifty shares in Ford Motor Company.

Sound like a bad deal? Not at all. Although it may look as if the Dodge brothers did all the putting up in return for a promise of paper, that paper multiplied in value for sixteen years until they sold it back to Ford in 1920 for $25 million. Another shareholder was not so fortunate. Albert Strelow, owner of a woodworking business, refurbished his two-story workshop to become Henry's manufacturing plant, adding $5,000 of his money to the kitty in return for fifty shares. Unfortunately, he thought he had a better idea, sold out early in the game, and reinvested in a gold mine, which didn't pay off like the Ford Motor Company. Either of these original shareholders could have put the package together if they had had the prime ingredient: the idea (always worth more than materials or money). Henry not only held the winning card but had the know-how to play it. He originated, planned, produced, and sold a winner, using other people's money, materials, and equipment; retaining control; and eventually owning the company outright by using its profits to buy out the other shareholders.

Early auto dealers maintained a stable out back—oftentimes a cattle yard—in case cars didn't catch on, and they traded farm implements, horses, and cows for each other as well as the new-fangled horseless carriages.

Even today there are many ways to get a free car. Automobile dealers barter cars for services; and cars are used by other companies as fringe benefits or in place of money to close a deal. Dealers may welcome an offer that helps them to cope with the problem of excess inventory. One dealer took an airplane, oil leases, equipment, cows, and chickens as partial trade on new cars. If you have ever traded in an old car on a new one, you know how to take the first step.

If you are a salesman (either full- or part-time) for a car dealer, you automatically receive the use of a car. Many federal, state, and civil employees are given a car for business because it is easier to rectify the purchase of a car on the books than to grant salary increases. True, many cars can be used only during working hours or to and from work, but if you travel a great deal or live at a distance from work, the savings can be considerable. In such an arrangement you save not only the initial investment but also maintenance costs and taxes.

If your employer will not give you a car as part of your employment contract, ask to be reimbursed for mileage on yours. You may receive more money this way, but if you do, report excess as income on your tax return. You will also be entitled to deduct interest on payments, and if you keep your car for over three years you can start deducting investment credit: after three years, one-third of 10 percent of the original cost; after five years, two-thirds of 10 percent; and after seven years, 10 percent of the cost; so if your car cost $6,000, you will eventually receive a tax credit of $600 from the government.

How else can you get a free car? Be a salesman for a product and use a company car. Or, if you work for a franchise that travels extensively in a specific area (like Welcome Wagon), go to a dealer there and sell him on the idea of donating a free car for your use in return for his advertisement printed on its side. As an instructor in driver education (either private or public) you will be given the use of a car because school systems and companies have found that training cars are safer parked at home than on public property.

If you can sell at least $240,000 worth of Mary Kay Cosmetics (home office in Dallas, Texas) you can win a pink Cadillac (with a one-year lease renewable on a year-to-year basis if your sales curve continues in the right direction). If you own an advertising agency, newspaper, radio or TV station, theater, hotel, or any other business dispensing a service needed by an automobile dealer, a free car can be worked into the business agreement.

No money changes hands. Each transaction is carried on the books as a trade-out or account receivable (then charged off to expenses), with cars later sold as demonstrators. Most deals are worked out on a six-month trial basis, often on a handshake or after a "Let's sit down and talk about it" session. Dealers usually prefer to do such business on a one-to-one basis, but if what they need is not available locally, they sometimes use a media broker (see Business of Barter). Larger dealers prefer using TV station advertising, but smaller agencies generally opt for radio.

"It's important to be selective," said one medium-sized dealer who keeps at least a dozen new models of his fleet earmarked for such transactions, "because these deals cost money although none is exchanged. You must select the theater whose patrons are most likely to drive your brand of car, or the radio station with the largest number of listeners in your area (usually a twenty-five-mile radius). I try to avoid oversaturation, and if I think I'm getting the short end of the stick, I can always ask for more advertising or fringe benefits, or back out completely." He keeps track of mileage and upkeep, which he measures against returns. At the current time he has cars bartered to two radio stations, one TV channel, a parts dealer, a newspaper, a drivers' education program, a gas station, a furniture store, a dinner theater, and a nationally known football player. The radio and TV stations and the newspaper barter advertising for their cars. The parts dealer sells at cost and gets free repairs on his personal and business cars. The furniture store owner supplies furniture for the car dealer's showroom and home. The drivers' education program provides advertising throughout the country and is chalked up to community service. The gas station is given leasing credit in return for gas charged by the dealer.

The dinner theater pays in several ways. The dealer is given free ads in the theater program; the theater in turn plugs the dealer in its radio ads. It also allows him blocks of tickets which he gives away on his radio program and in weekly drawings at his showroom. "Giving away tickets brings prospective customers into the showroom who would not come otherwise. If I back this up with aggressive salespeople, my percentage of sales from this source can run quite high. Such transactions are renewable or cancelable. If I think that a barter is not working out or not bringing in enough business, the agreement can be broken with a thirty-day notice."

The football player, in return for his free set of wheels, gives the dealer four season passes (which he can use himself or give away), makes personal appearances at special sales events, and invites the dealer to "in" events at the Touchdown Club, where the dealer is only too happy to pick up the tab in return for being included.

"It's good barter when both parties derive benefit," the dealer says, "but bad when only one party does; and really bad when no one does."

If you are bartering for a new car, it helps to know the average percentage in mark-ups. On economy cars, it is around 20 percent; standard, 25 percent; luxury, 27 percent; on each extra, close to 50 percent.

Partial deals are also made on a regular basis. A shopowner or restaurateur can work out a mutual advertising pact with a car dealer to lease a car at a reduced rate, depending on the value of the service exchanged. Most dealers prefer short deals to long. If your service is of a lesser nature, needed on a regular basis, or one needed on an irregular basis, you can work out terms for a used car or pay partially for a new one. A house painter received the use of a truck for a year in return for painting the buildings (the dealer bought the paint). Other dealers negotiate car leases and sales for services that include outdoor maintenance, indoor cleaning, insurance, medical and dental bills, rent, and so on.

If you are in a job where you meet a great many people, work for a large company, or work in a gas station servicing many people and cars, you can become a "bird dog." This term is used by automobile dealers and garage owners to describe people who send them customers ($4 to $25 a name and information) or give them tips that result in a straight sale with no trade (often $100) or a regular percentage of the sale or discount on their repair bill. Some bird dogs take cash, others accumulate credit toward a new car or to pay repair bills. Whichever route you choose, the terms must be worked out in advance, preferably in writing to protect yourself, although some dealers prefer that all deals remain oral and confidential.

Being a bird dog provides fringe benefits not available to other customers. If you become a profitable channel for new business, you may be able to arrange to do your own repairs in someone else's garage, obtain parts at wholesale, or get 10 to 20 percent off your repair bills.

Youngsters making soapbox derby cars who find themselves

short on funds can find a local merchant to sponsor them in a race who will pay all costs of making the car and, if the race is in another city, transportation also, in return for painting his advertising along the side. Some smaller towns do not sponsor soapbox derbies, and by the time a youngster does all the work involved, paying the freight can be a financial hardship. One of our sons found the perfect sponsor—a local furniture store, which, because it discounted prices, was not allowed to advertise in Washington. The store was delighted to pay the cost of construction, have its sign painter print the name along the side of the car, and even deliver it to the race in a company truck.

Stock car racers can use the same kind of barter to offset the high cost of repairs between races by finding a car dealer or automotive parts or machine shop to sponsor them. The dealer, in return for advertising on the sides of the car, provides parts. The racer does his own repairs and has access to the facilities of a professional shop. The expenses are usually washed out by the dealer with the costs obtained wholesale, and billed retail. Everyone comes out a winner.

Teen-agers who have already gained the use of the family car by doing errands, washing and waxing the car on a regular basis, or taking it in to the garage for checkups and repairs can expand their market and wheels by offering the same deal to neighbors or elderly citizens. A young man or woman can exchange baby-sitting in return for the use of a friend's car (usually on a two-to-one basis).

Automobiles can also be obtained through a one-time swap or service. Smaller repair shops will trade service for things like cameras, musical instruments, good used parts, plowing, firewood, bookkeeping, even flying lessons. Carpenters often exchange hours for engine work (with the receiver always paying for parts). If your car is old and parts are difficult to get, trade a service to a junk dealer in return for a car of the same vintage, which you can then use for extra parts. Or, if you have a friend skilled at car repairs, arrange a trade with him in return for his finding and fixing a used car.

If you patronize self-service gas stations, you are already bartering your time for a saving in the price. Many neighborhood gas stations barter gas on a regular basis for services and goods. Nelson Way, who owned a gas station in Pennsylvania during the Depression, took in apples, antiques, and insurance for gas, learned enough about antiques to write a book (*Antiques Don't Lie*, Doubleday), and thirty years later cashed in the insurance policies for an early retirement to buy an antique business. Gas stations in low-income neighborhoods often sell new tires at cost in order to get used tires, which are easier to sell to regular customers. Regular patronage at almost any tire dealer will put you in line for discounts.

In any phase of the automobile business (buying, leasing, gas, tires), there are two rules to remember. The best deals can be made at times when business or sales are low; and the figures used to add up to the transaction don't always have to represent money.

Babysitting

Barter Is Child's Play

Your children's time may be more valuable than you think. Someone else's needs can mesh with your need for time to yourself and, once you investigate possible free babysitting arrangements to make sure your child will be cared for competently, you can enrich your child's education while you take a day off. High schools and colleges have nursery schools for which they need workers. And those that don't, should . . . tell them. Volunteer to round up some young people to start one. Red Cross classes on child care often need to borrow a baby or small child for live demonstrations. Child psychology classes, too, observe (or, from your point of view, babysit) children. In the bargain, your offspring receive free play therapy which could save them years on the couch. Art and photography classes can always use models, teaching your children patience while immortalizing them. Senior citizens' homes are delighted to "share" regular visits with a child.

Even if nobody but you particularly needs your children, you must have something a potential babysitter would eagerly exchange. A music student without a piano might appreciate using yours in exchange for child care. Parlay your barter into piano lessons as the child gets older. Your backyard could be just the garden plot someone needs, in which case you could set up a schedule of babysitting to coordinate with planting and weeding (see Food). Lend your washing machine to an apartment dweller, your kitchen to a small-scale baker, your book collection or your sewing machine to suitable addicts. Find someone who needs part-time office space or a telephone-answering service. What better way to build barter credits than by answering the phone while you make peanut butter sandwiches or rock your infant? Since all the above are on your premises, your children become used to the babysitter, and vice versa. Decide whether you want the babysitting done at your home (often more acceptable to the child and easier for the parent) or theirs (which leaves you free to clean the house or treat yourself to a morning of reading in bed).

When summer comes, find the two most energetic and patient unemployed teen-agers in your neighborhood and offer your playroom, garage, basement, or yard for them to start a play group. Their rent is free in return for tuition for your children. Be sure the teen-agers provide playthings rather than relying entirely on those belonging to your children, or your offspring will feel they have gotten the short end of the bargain, and right they will be. They are never too young to learn to barter advantageously.

The ideal babysitter is someone who is as familiar to the child as a member of the family; who is there when the parents want to go out, but disappears when they are around so that their privacy is not invaded. You can attract one of these for yourself once you arrange a spare room and establish a few rules. Look in college housing offices, in classified ads under Rooms Wanted, or in an office where people work part-time (or any office at all if you need only evening and weekend babysitting). Interview, ask for references, and choose your babysitter by instinct. It has to be somebody you could bear to see passing through your kitchen on a frantic Monday morning. To set the rate, answer a few ads for furnished rooms to learn how yours compares. Then find out the highest local babysitting rate (you want your babysitter to feel valued) and calculate how many hours your room is worth. Establish from the first moment the rules that are comfortable for you: whether or not the sitter can use your living room, your evening newspaper, your telephone; whether and when guests are welcome; whether drinking and smoking are objectionable to you; whether there are hours you don't want the TV on or showers running. Establish whether your washer, television, linens, and such are to be used. Specify that the sitter must be responsible for keeping his or her quarters clean. Do you want to share your kitchen or provide separate cooking quarters? These can be as simple as a small refrigerator, a portable oven, and an electric frying pan. Better yet, cadge an old stove and refrigerator when somebody is redoing a kitchen and install them in your basement.

Talk about the rules your children have. The roomer/sitter should be expected to build up a proper relationship with the children. That means greeting and playing with them at times when he or she is not babysitting. It means being responsible for their welfare, caring enough to see that dinner consists of more than ice cream, enforcing bedtimes. Play up the parental role. Sell your babysitter on the chance to mold character and build a better world by encouraging your children to clean their rooms and finish their homework. The more interdependent your children and babysitter become, the better. One roomer/sitter was persuaded by the children to share the expense of a skateboard. It was obviously to his advantage to keep it in good condition, and he now spends time, when not sitting, taking turns on the skateboard.

Set up a babysitting schedule ahead or do it on a weekly basis. If the babysitter has to cancel out at the last minute, it is his responsibility to find a substitute. Arrange that if the children are asleep and the sitter is staying at home anyway, you can go out without chalking up hours. Discuss vacations. If the babysitter takes a trip, you should get either cash reimbursement or extra hours some other week. And specify that the arrangement requires two weeks' notice on either side to terminate it.

Do unto babysitters as you would have them do unto your children. Praise them. Let them know what they are doing right. Let your children know that when the babysitter is in charge, he is the court of last resort. Sprinkle your relationship with goodwill credits such as: Is there anything you need at the store? Would you like a piece of the cake I just baked? How did you get the children to arrange the blocks so neatly?

Once you have amassed a certain amount of expertise in baby-sitting barter, or if you prefer not to have a babysitter who lives in, then the next logical step is a cooperative sitting service. There are two kinds of babysitting co-ops (and by that we don't mean successful and unsuccessful). One sort is a simple barter—a very personal kind of system in which members call each other and ask for help, each member keeping track of what he or she owes. Books may be kept by a rotating secretary, perhaps with each month's secretary getting a free hour of babysitting. The system is kept informal, with as few mechanisms and rules as possible, and depends on a spirit of cooperation coupled with a sense of honor. Often the small, informal babysitting cooperative either grows from or becomes a social group, which makes the exchange complicated when all the members are invited to the same party. On the other hand, the babysitters, being friends and neighbors, are familiar to the children.

It sounds idyllic, and in some ways it is. But such co-ops, like children, are bound to reach an awkward adolescence when they have a growth spurt and need to cope with their unaccustomed maturity. The dozen members grow to forty; the original children explode into the teens, and the rough spots in the organization are no longer smoothed by a cup of coffee. A lot of rules are set up, often after very heated meetings, and the original members begin to feel like strangers in an organization they thought of as their baby.

In any case, once the co-op system becomes large and official, more ground rules are needed. Some co-ops initiate a scrip system, with each half hour worth one ticket and a strict limit on how many hours a member may owe. Some co-ops, if they are large enough to absorb a few losses of hours, issue new members thirty hours of scrip upon joining, requiring (with varying success) that the hours be paid back when the member leaves the group. Scrip is often paid double after midnight and during the dinner hour (5:00 to 7:00 P.M.). Saturday evening sits are paid an extra hour. The secretary is paid in scrip. If a parent returns late, there is a penalty in scrip. Daytime sitting may be paid more or less than evening sitting, large families more than small. Some co-ops use scrip for services over and above babysitting, like sewing Halloween costumes or driving children to school.

Beyond the rates of exchange, the co-op must decide how sitters are to be selected. Some prefer to have each member call a sitter; others transmit exchanges through a secretary whose job is to fill requests. In a large co-op, that becomes more efficient in dealing with special needs or unavailable evenings and helps distribute the demand, but does not guarantee familiar sitters for the children, requiring more compensation for the secretary.

A co-op often makes rules about where the sitting is to be done (for example, the child goes to the sitter during the day and the sitter to the child at night). It may require references for new members, even allowing or requiring departing members to pay debts in cash. Geographical boundaries are desirable. It may be useful to establish a co-op within the co-op, such as a rotating or hired-from-the-outside group of sitters for New Year's Eve or football games. The greatest problem? Deciding who will take care of the children while all the parents are busy setting up the rules!

Big Business

Purchasing World, a trade magazine, estimates that 48 percent of all U.S. companies large enough to employ a purchasing agent engage in some form of barter.

Fish breeders swap varieties; radio and TV stations trade advertising time for hotel space, theater tickets, and trips; dealers trade routes. Small department stores barter space in their windows to jewelers in return for accessories for mannequins and fashion shows. Large department stores give floor space to wine and cheese merchants for a percentage of their sales. Trendy department stores stage elegant openings to benefit charities in return for their mailing lists.

Universities trade computer time for furniture, tuition for advertising credits, and free admission to children of professors instead of pay increases. Businessmen exchange professional services on a regular basis or in return for needed favors. An investment counselor, after giving free advice to a media man, accepts his credit card on a trip to Europe. Having charged the agreed amount, the investment man returns it to the client, who deducts it as a business expense (see Media).

Large companies barter from stockpiles in order to procure needed materials in times of shortages and at other times to reduce excess stock or cut down on inventories not immediately usable, which in turn lowers interest costs and conserves capital investment. Dow Chemical Company ships ethylene to processors who cannot get it in exchange for a percentage of the manufactured polyethylene, which they need to supply their customers. Monogram Industries buys steel pipe it does not use to trade for phenol, needed in its insulating materials. Bartering has become so commonplace among American firms that the IRS is taking a hard look at barter deals to see how it can get a piece of the action.

Barter, known among businessmen as effective nonuse of cash, is used to conserve capital. The bartered asset can be something tangible such as inventory or something intangible such as talent or professional capability. Every business barters in one way or another. A car dealer who has a farm may furnish a farm equipment dealer with cars and trucks in exchange for the machinery he needs. No money changes hands, only goods. Swapping assets saves on the normal profit margin the other person would make. Neither shows a profit, yet each gets the assets he needs.

Business reputation, salesmanship, and know-how combined with a new idea can effect powerful barters. Sam Wyly started selling computer time to universities in the same way that power companies sell electricity. In 1963 when he founded University Computing, he wanted to buy a used computer. When he couldn't find a bank to finance the purchase, he negotiated an agreement whereby he would supply Southern Methodist University with computing time in exchange for housing the computer he planned to get on their campus. He then sold a five-year service contract to Sun Oil's research department for lower than the normal price in return for Sun Oil's prepayment of the contract, or $250,000 in cash. With no net worth he found a leasing company that would buy a used Control Data computer for $650,000 and lease it back to him. The deal was guaranteed by a Dallas company in exchange for a 49 percent interest. Sam paid the rent, became the majority stockholder, and later in his career acquired control of Bonanza Steak Houses.

Administrative skills can be parlayed through barter into ownership, stock options, or cash. Using talent to reorganize and redirect a company, an executive can gain 50 percent ownership or more (depending on his original contract) and go on to become president, taking control of the company without putting a penny down.

Formulas, patents, and mineral rights are traded in return for a percentage of sales, part ownership, stock, money, and land. Smart inventors keep control of a good idea and lease out its manufacture. Marvin Glass, who invented the "Mr. Machine" toy in 1960, sells no idea outright, leasing it instead to toy manufacturers for a percentage of the gross. Sometimes the only way to get a patent into production is by bartering part ownership with a manufacturer. When a partner withdraws or retires from a business or partnership, he is sometimes bought out with stock, assets, a seat on the stock exchange, joint use of a formula or the name of a product, or even the employment of relatives. Companies give stock options to executives, instead of raises, by which employees can buy stock at a lower price and either keep it for long-term capital gain or sell for immediate profit. Large companies buy up smaller ones, using stock as collateral—a good deal for the small company when the stock market is low and goes up, but bad if the market is high at purchase time and later falls.

Putting two needs together and being the middleman in the barter pays off. Fruit brokers contract orchards and find buyers, sometimes ending up with more money than those who do the growing and selling. One of the most famous bankers in America, A. P. Giannini, solicited deposits from Italian immigrants and farmers while simultaneously advertising for borrowers in foreign-language newspapers. His ingenuity paid off: after one and a half years nearly $2 million was deposited in his Bank of Italy in San Francisco.

James Ling was an electrician who thought big. He issued 800,000 shares of common stock in his company, Ling Electric Incorporated, kept 400,000, and sold the rest door-to-door for $2.25 each, raising $750,000 in working capital. He then bought another electric firm for cash which immediately raised the value of Ling stock. From that point he swapped stock to gain additional companies.

The seventh largest server of food in the United States, McDonald's, was started in 1954 with another form of barter. When Ray Kroc, a Chicago-based distributor of multimixers (a machine that mixes five malts at one time), checked out a San Bernardino restaurant run by Dick and Mac McDonald that was using eight multimixers, he was amazed to see people standing in line for 15¢ hamburgers. He figured that if he could talk the owners into opening more restaurants, he would sell more multimixers. Dick McDonald was a satisfied man who didn't want to leave home, so the McDonalds agreed to let Kroc franchise outlets for ½ of 1 percent of gross receipts. (Most people find it difficult to refuse something for nothing, especially if someone else is doing the work.) Six years later, in 1961, Kroc bought the contract name, all trademarks, copyrights, and formulas from the McDonalds for $2.7 million. Today, a McDonald's franchise costs six figures to lease equipment and provide operating capital. In addition to the initial investment, McDonald's selects the site and builds the restaurant, collecting a 3 percent service fee and 8.5 percent rent from monthly sales after deducting sales tax; 60 to 70 percent of the owner-operators are millionaires. An average outlet grosses between $430,000 to $500,000 annually, and an operator can make as much as $50,000 to $70,000 in annual profits.

If one has a good idea or product but lacks advertising funds, bartering for exclusive sales rights in an area may do the trick. In 1948 the makers of Polaroid Camera launched their product nationwide with no sales organization by offering one department store in each city a thirty-day exclusive, provided the store would advertise prominently in newspapers and promote the cameras throughout the store. The demand was so great that salesmen were selling floor models without parts; one year later sales were close to $7 million.

Getting a corner on the market also helps. When TV stations didn't want to carry underwear advertising, Playtex bought up a huge library of old films which they offered free to stations in return for running ads. If the stations wanted the movies, it was the only way they could get them.

If you can find a new way around an old problem and use the idea to barter for capital, you may come up a winner. Daniel Ludwig, who has the world's largest private shipping fleet (greater than Aristotle Onassis's or Stavros Niarchos's), originally owned one tanker chartered to an oil company. He wanted to buy an old general cargo ship and convert it to an oil tanker (because oil paid more than dry cargo) but he didn't have the money. Having gotten a contract from an oil company, he used charter fees as monthly payments on the loan he needed by assigning the charter to the bank. It collected the fees directly from the oil company until the loan was repaid. Essentially, Ludwig used the oil company's credit rating to improve his own. As soon as he converted the tanker, he took the formula one step further. He designed a ship for a special purpose, found a customer to charter it before the keel was laid, then deferred payment on the loan. The bank expected little or no money until it was afloat—an avant-garde idea at the time that caught on and is now practiced by many others.

In other barters, rights to minerals are kept separate from land exploration expenditures during the development or production stages and their value deducted later. Development costs are deductible and can be deferred until a mine starts producing, offsetting profits at that time. Mineral rights are leased in return for a percentage of the output, or a straight lease for money. Other companies grubstake mining ventures for a fifty-fifty split.

On a smaller scale, one woman who couldn't afford the rent to start an office service borrowed $600 from a bank and opened a serve-yourself office for others who needed office space part-time or full-time. Many out-of-towners in need of a city address or burdened with commuting and telephone costs found the $25-a-day space charge attractive enough to sign contracts guaranteeing them one day a week on a regular basis. The arrangement was also a plus for salesmen and writers who previously had to keep two residences or offices. They can now live in the country and commute only once a week to their offices.

"Over half our business comes through implied barters," confided the executive of a nationwide consulting firm. "They are sometimes discussed openly, but they are always understood by both parties. For instance, we might conduct a management seminar for a client at a reduced fee with the understanding that he will invite prospective clients, in effect bringing to us people who would be interested in our service, saving us the cost of contacting them ourselves and then trying to generate interest on their part. Actually, it can work either way. In one of our company management training programs, a company put it right on the line to us in the negotiations by saying, 'Give us a good price and we'll invite the right people from nearby cities.' Sometimes nobody brings it up at all because we know whom they will invite. On seminars for one public works association we barely make expenses, but their membership is made up of county commissioners and engineers from all over the country. It's the best free advertising we've got.

"We also use a client's facilities in lieu of a fee: free office space, telephone, reproduction machines, cars for transportation, and we're not paying taxes on that as income. It doesn't cost them anything because these are facilities they are paying for anyway. Colleges and universities even furnish us with a secretarial staff. Our contract spells out what facilities we will receive free, but it never shows up in the accounting records.

"Working this way pays off at other levels. Say a client retains us to improve the productivity of his operation. Normally when we're finished with the assignment (a year or eighteen months), those engineers and managers who have worked with us will be the top administrators in the organization. Word gets around."

Sometimes the word boomerangs. A Virginia firm leased a bingo hall for $2,000 a month including utilities, then leased it to a boys' club to conduct bingo five nights a week, charging the organization for complete remodeling of the building, installation of 10 tons of air conditioning, equipment purchase, maintenance and janitorial services. After taking in $138,129 in five months, the boys' club received only $19,624 because "rent" averaged $11,574 a month. The "middleman" is now being investigated by authorities.

In some barters there is a fine line between business and influence-peddling, determined, in many cases, only by going to court. Until recent years much of this has gone uncontested, but since Watergate, there has been a flood of investigations by government agencies, grand juries, and private groups such as the Organization for Consumer Justice. If someone offers you something for nothing, there is often a string attached. In the media there is a saying that the difference between legal and illegal dealings is that "one is on top of the table and the other is under it." If you win a contract, a position on a governing board, or even the franchise for selling lottery tickets because of your experience and/or location and feel free to talk about the details, the chances are you have earned it. However, if there is the slightest question in your mind from the outset, ask questions of the person making the offer *before* you get involved; afterwards, someone else may be asking the questions of *you*.

If you have a good idea and the ability to put it across, the business world is a fine arena in which to try it. Play in your own league until you have enough practice to match wits with those who have more experience than you. Research your idea from all angles to make sure you know all the answers. Play your cards close to your chest until the time is right.

Then, when someone asks you, "Whose business is this anyway?" it may be yours.

See also: Autos; Business of Barter; Housing; Land, Real Estate, and Mineral Rights; Media; Sex.

Books, Magazines, and Newspapers
So That's Why They Call Them Trade Books

What makes magazines and newspapers so barterable is that using them doesn't use them up. Rarely do you use them more than once, yet they remain valuable to someone who has not yet read them. And each publication you can trade off with someone else costs half as much.

The easiest book exchange is, of course, your neighborhood lending library. Some libraries or other community gathering places set up a used-book exchange, whereby you bring a used book and choose one from the shelves in return. Or you bring books whenever you have them and take one whenever you want it.

New books are another matter. Publishers do exchange books, usually for publicity. So your challenge is to convince the publisher that your reading their book will sell copies. If you are a publisher—and we hope some of our readers are—you can trade your books for another publisher's books; it is done all the time. Short of starting a small press, you can get free books from a publisher's publicity department if you are a person with influence over book buyers.

If you have connections with a TV or radio station and can get an author onto a talk show, that is good for one or several books. Authors have even bartered for a better time slot by offering more books.

College professors have a sure-fire bookselling technique: they assign books to their students. Thus, publishers are happy to send free books to teachers of pertinent subject matter, particularly when those teachers work for large universities. Carried to its ultimate implication, professors of introductory courses in large universities have major selling points in finding a publisher for their own books.

But getting a Ph.D. and a teaching job is a roundabout, not to mention expensive, way of qualifying for free books. On a simpler level, you may be in line for free gardening books if you were presenting a seminar or building a gardening library for your club. The head of a nursery school book group can ask for a publisher's titles on preschool children. Whatever your interest, find a group of like-minded people with whom to review or discuss books and ask a publisher to provide you with review copies, promising to sell copies of the books at your meetings. Or organize a book fair.

Publishers often give books to charities as tax deductions. Hospitals, senior citizen centers, and school rummage sales are all eligible.

Publishers have been known to pay for services (to artists, architects, exterminators) in books. Bookstores sometimes pay for services in black and white rather than green. If all else fails, become a friend or business acquaintance of a publisher or reviewer. An extreme step, of course, but what else do you think they give as Christmas gifts?

As for getting free magazines, schoolchildren of earlier days knew they could get a subscription to their favorite magazine by selling subscriptions and earning points. Or they could earn a football and all sorts of treasures the magazine company itself probably got in barter. New magazines will trade copies for all kinds of things they need, including manuscripts and subscribers. Countless writers started their careers by writing in exchange for free copies or subscriptions to a magazine. Many new magazines take free subscribers to boost subscription numbers in order to get higher advertising rates, and more advertisers. Barter companies list the magazines (everything from *Atlantic Monthly* to *Writer's Digest*) that will trade subscriptions for merchandise or services. Magazine subscriptions are given as prizes in magazine puzzle contests and for contributing names of new subscribers. If you buy subscriptions as gifts for four friends, you can often get one free. Check the price on gift subscriptions. If it is lower than that for a regular subscription, bargain with a friend to renew each year in the other one's name. *Mother Earth News* gives a free subscription to anyone sending in a barter anecdote it can use.

Free newspaper subscriptions can be had in return for writing a local column or being a regular neighborhood or area correspondent. High school students can make this barter pay off doubly if their writing evokes a response from the public. Because editors like to sell newspapers, such students will be first in line for full-time summer jobs. Using both forms of experience in college applications, they'll also increase their chances at bartering their way into journalism school. Teachers of current events or journalism are often entitled to free newspaper subscriptions delivered daily to the classroom by simply writing to an editor and saying they would like to use the publication as a good example of news coverage.

The problem remains: how can you get a free copy of this book? Make us an offer.

The Business of Barter

Barter is a booming business in the United States, with sales and exchanges totaling over $13 billion a year. Although a large amount of this is in real estate transfers, an increasing percentage represents local and national bartering agencies. These range in size from regional credit card computerized exchanges to Atwood Richards, Inc., one of the leaders in what has come to be known as the reciprocal trade industry, which handled close to $100 million worth of goods and services during 1976 alone.

The $13 billion does not include barter fairs and shops, galleries, and private businesses, trading with each other to avoid spending cash, for convenience, or to dispose of surpluses. Some barter shops charge a small membership fee to trade off what members don't want whenever they see something they do. When a membership fee does not exist, 10 to 30 percent of the value of the exchange is paid in cash. Some exchanges specialize in appliances; others in wedding gifts or exclusively in children's merchandise. A San Francisco art gallery has a corner of paintings that can be bartered for with goods and services.

The Northeast Washington Barter Fair moves to a different location each year for its October camp-in of barterers, who come from all over the Northwest to trade seeds, medicinal herbs, musical instruments, crafts, raw materials, semiprecious stones, food (cooked and raw), grains, and in 1975, over 2 tons of honey. Operating on the theory that no amount is too small or too large, they truck in water, cooperatively cook meals, and even recycle trash after the event. For further information write: Rural Resources and Information, New Jerusalem Meadows, Tonasket, Washington 98855.

USE (Useful Services Exchange) is a pioneering pilot project being developed to improve the quality of life in Reston, Virginia. Organized for neighbors to help each other on a volunteer basis, the nonprofit, nonmonetary group offers a community-wide pool of over 100 person-to-person services on an hour-for-hour basis on which any member of the community may draw, including tutoring, music lessons, cooking, and sharing freezer space. With 360 registered participants, donated office space and equipment, it is operated by 11 office workers who work for credit hours. Through a rapid retrieval system, a person needed to fill a particular service can be located in a matter of seconds. Records of all transactions, services offered and requested, plus the current balance for each participant, are recorded. Each time someone calls, parties agree on the amount of labor time earned and report this to the clearinghouse. A special account of donated credit hours has been set up for the use of feeble elderly and handicapped residents faced with urgent needs.

The membership of The Learning Exchange in Evanston, Illinois, with 24,000 participants (see Education) is growing by more than 1,200 new members a month, with an information bank of 60,000 file cards listing names and telephone numbers of students and teachers under 3,000 headings from sports to classical subjects. Other barter cooperatives are formed to swap houses so that members enjoy free vacation residences (see Vacations).

The Service Exchange (3534 S.E. Main, Portland, Oregon 97214) applied for and received a contract with the City of Portland under the Comprehensive Employment Training Act, in May 1975. With this grant they are able to pay salaries for three full-time employees and one part-time college work/study person. Maintaining a file of some 1,200 people interested in trading what they do for someone else's services, they help on the average of 250 people a month. Open from 9:00 A.M. to 9:00 P.M. Monday through Thursday and until 6:30 P.M. Friday, they carry every imaginable skill from bagpipe playing to dentistry. Because Pacific Northwest Bell has a phone system that allows more than two people to converse at the same time, the Service Exchange can introduce two prospective barterers via phone and let them work out the details without giving them each other's names and phone numbers. Records are kept on each applicant, call, and arrangement made, with a donation equivalent to 10 percent of the exchange requested from each individual to develop a source of funding so that they can eventually become self-supporting.

The Lane County Exchange System in Oregon trades goods and services. A semiannual journal listing businesses interested in making trades is sent to subscribers for $9 a month, and $54 is charged for each listing in the journal. The system has two types of trades: short-term, when services or goods are exchanged in a short time period; or when one or both traders receive credit in each other's businesses. For example, if a lawyer needed a car, he would grant the car dealer the sales amount in legal services.

Smaller operations charge a $3 registration fee, plus $3 from each person on each transaction ($6 for a match), selling a monthly mimeographed list of available barters for $2. Others pool businesses in a certain area and issue coupon books. The West Wind Coupon Saver's Club (1271 Coral Way, Miami, Florida 33145) trades coupons you don't want for those you do, if you send them $3.50 a year membership with a list of what you prefer. For every $3 worth of coupons plus 60¢ handling, they will send you $3.60 in coupons.

The 300 members of The Business Owners Exchange in Minneapolis pay a $150 membership fee, trading professional services as well as personal goods and real estate. Functioning like a bank clearinghouse, issuing checks that look like commercial bank checks, and sending members monthly statements, members pay retail prices, plus a 7 percent service charge each month. Businessmen who belong say it brings in additional business that would not otherwise be solicited because although professionals cannot advertise, they can refer clients to one another.

The United Trade Club in San Jose, California, with 1,700 members, has a computer to keep track of offers, transactions, and credits, placing a limit on the amount of credit available to each member (usually $1,000 to $1,500). Once a member reaches his limit, his name is placed on a reserve list until his account is balanced. This list is mailed with the monthly statement. When a shopowner reaches his maximum, he places a sign in his window to inform members that he may not accept their trade. As a safety valve, each member in good standing is issued a monthly sticker to attach to his card, so that if a member is behind in payments, he will not receive a sticker; other members, not seeing the monthly sticker, will not transact business with him.

Mutual Credit Buying System, Inc., a rapidly growing barter system in Los Angeles, does about $1 million worth of transactions each month. Its 3,500 members (who each pay $49.50 to join) receive credit cards, and transactions are computerized, with members paying a percentage in cash to cover expenses. A public trading corporation in business for six years and approved for franchising in fifty states, they also make loans up to $50,000. One member arranged for all the expenses of his wedding using "MCB Futures," including the chapel, ministerial fee, flowers, photographer, wedding dinner, and hotel accommodations. Another member paid $10,000 in futures as part of his divorce settlement; while another paid off the cost of cosmetic surgery and contact lenses by working as a legal secretary. Also available: births, funerals, and all the services necessary in between.

The largest bartering cooperative in America is California's Business Exchange, Inc., North Hollywood. Organized in 1960, it now has twenty-five participating franchise areas throughout the

United States. Operating like a bank, it lists 6,000 businesses on its roster. Its $175 initial fee includes $36 in first-year dues, in addition to an 8 percent accounting fee on monthly purchases. Many of its members prefer dealing on a 50 percent cash, 50 percent barter basis.

Firms specializing in arranging barters for restaurants and hotels are listed under Due Bills in the yellow pages.

A highly sophisticated version of barter exists in what is known as the reciprocal trade industry. One of the largest of these firms (already mentioned) is Atwood Richards, Inc., in New York City. Its board chairman, president, and chief executive, Moreton Binn, known as the Barter Baron, was previously head of a promotional agency dealing in contests, sweepstakes, and sales incentive programs (see Media). During the recession of the early 1970s when retailers, because sales were down, could not afford to buy advertising, Binn realized that opportunities existed at the other end of the business. Since then he has negotiated trades of everything from bat manure to jets for advertising space and hotel credits, with his annual gross now close to $100 million. With profits and leverage built into each transaction, only 80 to 90 percent of each transaction is passed along. The excess is sold through the company's merchandising department for cash. When a product may jeopardize sales stateside, it is sold overseas. What is not bartered for advertising credits may also be sold to large discount stores, or to banks and businesses as gifts and premiums, or Binn holds his own warehouse sales, selling everything at wholesale prices or less. At other times the company will produce quiz shows and personality specials, bartering the goods to channels for credit. The bartering helps manufacturers move inventory off shelves, conserve cash, and obtain advertising at the same time.

Before you join any barter organization, advise franchise specialists and make sure it comes under some kind of state regulations or is licensed, because national regulations are nonexistent. The Washington Trade Exchange is currently being investigated by U.S. postal authorities to determine if members were adequately warned of risks and if the exchange is complying with federal tax laws. A number of similar firms throughout the United States have collapsed in recent years. Individuals selling services can benefit

more than those selling goods because their money is not tied up
in inventory.

And before you join any barter group, there are a few questions
you should ask: What are your legal rights? How can you cash in
on your credits? Are they transferable? Can you give them away or
sell them? What if you die? Some members of commercial bartering firms have been unable to spend their credits except on dubi-
ous real estate, or were treated unjustly in some transactions; or a
listed member would not extend credit for one reason or another,
or raised prices after learning of a customer's membership. To offset such problems, one optometrist stopped exchanging his services on a 100 percent basis and compromised by providing glasses
to members who paid 75 percent cash.

Dick Kasdan, who formed a barter group in Washington, D.C.,
felt it failed because it became too time-consuming for most of its
members. The greatest problem was equalizing value, as a lawyer
might charge $50 an hour compared to a plumber's $18. Attorneys
concerned about malpractice often refuse to represent such groups
officially, preferring to be an adviser on an informal basis.

The Service Exchange in Portland cautions volunteers not to
bite off more than they can chew because it is better to say no than
to make commitments they can't keep. They also advise barterers
to trade names and telephone numbers so that if either cannot
keep an appointment, the other person will be informed; and
if a member reneges on a deal, they want to be the first to know. It
also helps, they advise, "to know exactly what each party is going
to do before you begin working. If, after starting, it looks like more
work may be necessary, stop and negotiate."

Clothing

The Shirt on Your Back

As costly as clothing is, to some people it is worthless. Outgrown or outdated clothing is lying around virtually every house, waiting for the right size or use.

Used clothing is a cinch to barter. Cultivate a friend whose children are a little older or bigger than yours. About one year in size is just right; if they are too much older, their clothing may be gone, outdated, or mildewed by the time your children have grown into it. The ideal time to strike a clothing barter is the moment the owner is faced with having to wrap and store it. Offer anything in trade—even as simple as taking it off their hands.

The same deal can be worked with friends who have gained or lost weight. Nobody wants to face clothes that don't fit. Save them the anguish; offer to clean out their closets and haul away discards. And don't overlook third-person trades: you may be the happy medium between a large and a little friend.

In Cambridge, Massachusetts, "Free Box" containers (3-foot by 5-foot bins with hinged lids) have been placed outside churches and inside stores for neighbors to put in discards; each one takes out what he wants. Beautiful Day, a health food store in College Park, Maryland, has a free clothing corner.

Moving north? Advertise your warm-weather clothes in a northern community to trade with someone moving south. Or trade your ski clothes to a neighbor the year you take a Caribbean cruise.

If you are traveling no farther than downtown, suggest to someone your size (in mid-season) that you switch wardrobes or ball gowns (or whatever else you are tired of wearing). You will both feel brand new and gain room in your closet at the same time.

New clothes, like any merchandise, can be traded for goods and/or services. Many a dentist trades bridgework to clothing retailers. Clothes can also be traded for publicity. Notice the screen credits of movies and TV shows: "Miss TV Star's Clothes by . . ." Television performers borrow wardrobes in exchange for the publicity. A talk show hostess might drop into a store once a week to exchange five outfits for next week's wardrobe. Some stores hire socialites to model for a luncheon, paying them with the outfits they model. If you appear publicly, offer your body to a clothing shop as a showcase for their merchandise. If you have a friend who is a silversmith or jeweler, and you go to large parties, save money in accessories by offering to model his latest creations at affairs where prospective customers are likely to lurk.

Don't be afraid to tackle the most elegant shops in town. Kitty Kelley coveted a Dior wedding gown far beyond her means, in a large, expensive downtown establishment. After stalking the department store's bridal shop, five visits, and fifteen phone calls, she finally persuaded the manager to reduce the price. The word *barter* was never mentioned; tact was vital. Clearly, the manager was intrigued by the pigtailed author dressed in Dr. Scholl sandals and T-shirt dreaming Dior. The price kept dropping until it was one-third the original. In a last-minute implied barter, Kitty invited the manager to her reception; and the manager invited Kitty to her home, where her friend did the alterations and made a copy of the $100 hat for a fraction of the price.

A barter that costs the store nothing is an agreement to give commission on referral sales. You buy your clothes and refer friends to the store when they admire your wardrobe. Even if you don't make a sale, you can depreciate the cost of your clothes on your income tax. Other stores (especially in small towns) have spring and summer fashion shows at the local theater or restaurant. Models chosen from the community often have a choice of one outfit or a discount all year.

Clothing barters are frequently unspoken; try to recall how many cartoons show a lascivious old man buying a fur coat for a sweet young thing. A more discreet unspoken barter occurs in the wholesale showrooms of New York's garment district. No one will go on record with this, but buyers from major department stores make a point of cultivating their own special salespeople and then place all future orders with them. If the department store's clothes do not sell fast enough within the first ten days, they call the wholesaler and exchange the losing style for one that has been selling well in other stores.

What finally happens to those unwanted styles? The same thing that happens to unwanted clothes in homes around the country. Whatever has no other outlet goes to the charity thrift shops or institutions—in exchange for tax deductions.

If you can't manage to work out a trade for ready-made clothes, consider custom-made. Dig out that priceless fabric your grandmother left you, or the brocade somebody brought you from Hong Kong. If there is enough for two garments, a seamstress or tailor can design yours in exchange for the unused half. And seamstresses need goods and services as much as anybody else . . . home-baked breads, child care, your old sofa. Even your old clothes, if they are made from highly valued fabrics, may be just what a tailor needs.

Major cities have shops that sell high-quality second-hand clothing; usually the shops are called something like Once Again, Encore, or Almost New. Trade your clothes for others, place them on consignment, and buy what you want from the profits, or offer to repair clothes in exchange for garments.

Whatever you want, shoes or hats, head for the top management to propose your deal. A children's shoe store may need small gifts to give its young customers, or a colorful mural for the wall, or a corner outfitted with your children's discarded toys to keep impatient children quiet. A men's store may need a tailor. A women's shop can use a talented person to devise window and wall displays, or emergency sales help. How about lunches brought in on Saturdays?

You say you've done all that and now you're ready for a mink and want to know how to get one? Well, there are always those sugar daddies; or you could trade labor to a mink farm; or why don't you just pick out the best label in town, go to that store, find the one that suits you, walk up to the manager, and ask, "How

long would it take to work this off? You see, I've just finished reading this new book on barter—and I was wondering what needs you
have that I could fill?"

If you're young and voluptuous, you may get one answer. But
even if you're not, you may find your talents can easily afford (or
be traded for) what's always been on your mind.

Crafts

Getting Potted

Crafts and craftsmen have all kinds of built-in barter systems. Although Rumplestiltskin gave the industry a bad name for a while
when, after spinning hay into gold for three nights, he demanded a
necklace, a ring, and the firstborn child in payment, barter has
flourished traditionally among craftsmen.

Some seek it, many encourage it, and most enjoy the thrill
(and sustenance) of the game. They trade off wares to friends and
strangers to increase art collections; to get food for the table; and
to help with the work, housing, space in kilns and studios, education, and crafts of other exhibitors at fairs.

As in other forms of barter, the first consideration in any trade is
value. If you are a prospective customer who would like to pay for
crafts with other goods or services, the easiest way to begin negotiations is by asking, "Would you like to trade?" If the other party
agrees, you then decide what you have of comparative value that
he is willing to accept.

"It's a great way to get things you couldn't otherwise afford,"
says Bruce Bartol, co-owner of South Mountain Pottery in Maryland, "or to acquire necessities without putting out cash. When
cost doesn't balance on both sides of a trade, one person sometimes adds cash, but most craftsmen prefer not doing so. I like to

get an agreement early in a craft fair," he says, "because if business is not as good as expected, craftsmen may not be willing to trade later on." On the other side of the coin, craftsmen who sell well are inclined to think their prices are due for an increase and not be as willing to trade; or if they do, they want cash as part payment. If Bruce expresses interest in what someone has but that person doesn't stop by his booth during a fair, he lugs some of his merchandise to the other person's area to see if he wants to trade. If the other person doesn't think the deal is equitable, Bruce adds more to his side. "Trading off this way is good advertising," he has discovered. "It distributes your crafts in new areas and more people see them." The biggest problem in closing a deal with another craftsman, he feels, is "the third party, the background person who isn't there: a husband who is going to give a wife hell if she comes home with more pots; or a partner who doesn't like to display other people's wares."

As a craftsman's reputation and price scale increase, barters are easier to arrange, more come his way, he in turn can expect more for his goods, and the arena for bartering his talent enlarges. He can apply for a grant from the National Endowment for the Arts. He can get a job teaching at the local college, having it furnish a workshop, materials, and apprentice as part of the arrangement. If he lives near a National Park, he may apply as a craftsman-in-residence, obtaining free studio space and utilities in return for setting up a regular schedule of classes (as is done at Glen Echo Park near Washington, D.C.). Some of these posts require craftsmen to give tours and do not permit living in, while other county and state parks, as well as house restorations, prefer a craftsperson to live on the premises and provide housing as part of the job.

Once a craftsman becomes established, he can barter for free help—otherwise known as an apprentice. In Europe apprentices must sign a contract for a minimum of two years, but in this country terms are usually arrived at through another form of barter. In return for learning a craft firsthand (and sometimes getting room and board as well), the apprentice helps with the labor, maintenance, errands, cleaning, packing, paperwork, administration, pricing, and transporting of crafts to market. Because competition is keen for apprenticeship posts, it helps an applicant to have marketable skills that will save the master's time—such as carpentry or electrical or writing talents. Although many craftsmen prefer doing everything themselves, production people need help, and their need outweighs problems. Stacking and loading a kiln can take as much as two days. After firing, shelves must be scraped and dipped, which again takes additional time. Each job that requires two days can be accomplished in one with two people working—a plus factor in meeting deadlines. Potters without kilns barter making clay, sifting glazes, and cleaning studio and kiln for space in the kiln during firing. Weavers trade fabric for help in threading looms.

Craftsmen barter wares for photography (needed for their applications to juried shows and also for advertising brochures); for newspaper ads or text for brochures; or in return for building fair displays. One craftsman worked out a deal with a carpenter by which he helped build a house on good days and the carpenter worked on his display space on bad days—inside. Another, a blacksmith, shoes horses at a racetrack in return for free housing and studio space. Potters with kilns trade firing space for labor, or crafts for new roofing materials. When craftsmen stay over with friends while making deliveries of stock, they usually pay for room and board with crafts of comparable value. They receive tickets to fairs after helping distribute literature and posters, or pay for editing a doctoral thesis with merchandise of the writer's choice.

Participating in weekend workshops sponsored by companies or in conjunction with educational institutions is another form of barter. In return for teaching, you can receive free materials, advertising, use of the facilities, and sometimes free tuition for other courses at the school. Potters who use dung firing swap labor or pots for manure; others pay for firewood with labor or crafts. If a merchant shares his downtown window to display crafts, he is paid with a percentage of what is sold. One potter worked out a deal with a company that rents plants to businesses. In return for selling decorator planters to the company at a reduced price, he persuaded the florist to advertise his pots, bringing both more orders.

Many craft shops trade floor space to craftsmen in return for waiting on counter or tending the cash register. If there is a health food store or restaurant connected with the operation, craftspersons can pay booth rent by waiting on tables, cooking, making store signs, or even painting advertisement posters for the sides of buses. After the Craftworks in Frederick, Maryland, opened The Deli restaurant, it became the most popular hangout in town. Although the restaurant found a folk singer for Friday and Saturday night entertainment, it needed a piano but lacked the cash. The owners placed an ad in the local newspaper: "Wanted, piano in trade for meal credits," figuring there must be a retired person in the neighborhood who would like to eat out while listening to someone else play.

One local craftsman, when confronted with the expense of surgery without medical insurance, took along slides of his pots when he went for his appointment to see his X-rays. After viewing the pots, the doctor tore up the artist's check, accepted the pots in payment for the surgery, and sold the anesthesiologist on the idea, too.

As business increases, craftsmen barter for additional help, sell shares in their business to other craftsmen, or barter space in their buildings, helping to pay off construction costs. Gordon and Diana Brott built a gallery in Camden, Maine, through barter. They traded sculpture, knitting, and weaving for carpeting, wood, windows, even shoes. Stephen Winter, a candlemaker in California, got into the habit of asking how people were fixed for candles each time he saw something he wanted. He discovered that if another craftsperson was doing well he bartered easily, but if the other was not doing well he hesitated, thinking that if he held off he might get money from someone else. But if he was doing very badly, he would barter because getting candles was better than nothing. Winter also established the Winter Rule from the experience. "Barter with the wealthy," he advises, "because if you hit it, you'll hit it big."

On the negative side of the scale, potters in residence sometimes find they end up with less than they bargained for, especially if the deal was not in writing; that interrupting work to conduct tours or sell souvenirs disrupts the flow of creative juices and may not offset the prestige address or the use of materials and facilities. Master craftsmen, despite the need to keep up with orders, lose patience with apprentices who don't keep their place, or craftsmen whose pots blow up in the kiln.

The bent to barter is an important leverage in the lives of craftsmen. They trade wares for quilts, furniture, house plans, rent, dentistry, vacations, old stoves (to convert to home kilns), use of a car, transportation, or publicity. When bartering with professionals, they usually decide beforehand the dollar value of the craft, then are allowed credit up to that amount.

Craftsmen are generally fair and objective when dealing with each other or with the public. But occasionally one thinks his work is worth more than you feel it is and a barter cannot be arranged no matter how many chips you stack on your side of the table. If you run into one who is too demanding or difficult to deal with, or who sees his hay as gold, the best way to end the dealing is to look him dead in the eye and shout, "Rumplestiltskin!" With any luck, he may stamp his foot and disappear through the floorboards.

Education

Trade Schools

Everything from learning how to plant seeds to receiving a doctorate is available through barter. The less formal the instruction, the less you have to barter for it. In fact, education is sometimes thrown in free as a by-product of something else.

For instance, if you have a garden that needs love and attention, and a child with an overabundance of time and an ignorance of horticulture, offer his help to the maintenance person. The job will get done twice as fast for half the money and the child will learn the difference between weeds and flowers. Or if a neighbor loves to garden, ask her to teach your child in her garden and let him practice in yours. Better still, ask her to revamp your landscaping with the help of your child in return for providing her with a service. Before long, your child will be contracting to do other yard work and your neighbor may be designing the town's botanical gardens.

In recent years, individuals recognizing that education is a function of living and an exchange of ideas, skills, and special areas of knowledge and expertise have formed learning exchanges throughout the United States. The Learning Community in Portland, Oregon, offers self-directed seminars on any subject in which interest is shown. They charge no instructors' fees, and a $5 registration fee covers the expense of the catalog. Terms are eight weeks long; instructors' fees may not exceed $25 per course or term; and barter to pay registration and course fees is encouraged.

The Learning Exchange in Evanston, Illinois, specializes in bartering skills. Referral service is free, although the exchange offers a $15 membership, part of which is tax-deductible, and half price for elderly and low-income people. Dues cover a subscription to the annual catalog, a quarterly newsletter, and a hotline phone number for members only. Contributions from corporations and foundations make up the rest of the revenue. Once the exchange puts its members in touch with one another, they are free to set up fee scales or bartering arrangements.

Swap-a-Skill at San Jose State University, California, lists over 200 skills and knowledge areas in which participating students are qualified to teach in return for being taught other skills. Participants report that second go-rounds are more rewarding than the first.

Early Jesuit records show that Patrick Henry learned French from John Dubois. After learning English from Patrick, Dubois went on to become one of America's first Catholic bishops. If you want to learn a foreign language, put up notices anywhere there are people who speak another language: grocery stores in ethnic neighborhoods, colleges, senior citizens' homes, community centers. Trade lessons in American life (grocery shopping, department store credit and banking skills, sightseeing, filling out forms) for language lessons. Offer a foreign or language student a meal and an evening of color TV per lesson, or take him or her into your home as boarder/barterer.

The greatest advantage of educational barters is that both parties have the commodity to barter again and again. It is a barter that reproduces itself endlessly. One form of educational barter that reproduced itself was Tevye's exchange in *Fiddler on the Roof*. By arranging to give Perchick meals for tutoring his daughters, Tevye got more than he bargained for: a son-in-law.

One of the first educational barters in our country was the apprenticeship system, whereby labor and a commitment for future work were exchanged for learning a trade (see Crafts). The process still continues, although a minimum wage is often paid as part of the bargain. Anything you want to learn that is being done in your community is available through a loose interpretation of this system. Find out who knows what you want to know (auto repair, harmonica playing, eggshell painting) and offer to do some of his dog work. Thus, while you are polishing chrome, making deliveries, or cleaning paintbrushes, you will be learning the process. Potter Carol Ridker takes on apprentices who are responsible for the janitorial services and maintenance in her studio. She has more time for pots, and the apprentices learn in the process.

Two students, Donna Brant and Peggy Clark, did some of the research for this book. While learning the ways of an author, they reduced our workload. In some cases colleges give course credit to student interns. If you have a business that can't keep up with its workload, contact the nearest school and see what kind of terms you can arrange. In exchange for exercise lessons, Karen Diamond's Figure Factory has accepted wardrobe consultation, public relations, ceramics, dried and fresh flowers, and calligraphy for invitations.

If there is a new cooking school opening near you, offer to do the dishwashing, telephoning, or shopping in exchange for lessons. Volunteer to put signs on bulletin boards for a piano teacher (piano teachers are notorious barterers), or ask if your child can get free lessons if you guarantee three more students. Drama schools, sewing classes, photography classes, all need some kind of service. If there is no class in what you want to learn, find your own expert. Offer to set up classes, finding students in return for free tuition. Trade off unused musical instruments to a teacher in return for music lessons.

Many libraries, companies, and educational institutions will provide free classrooms, instructors, publicity, and films if your course fits into their goal structure. Present your case, demonstrate a need, and they are often only too glad to assist. Some may videotape the course for further dissemination; others may give you an award so they can publicize their involvement.

A group of parents in Frederick, Maryland, formed the Catoctin Mountain Learning Project to educate children from preschool through third grade. They now own the school, sharing the administration and teaching as well. They salvage and collect construction materials for projects; sell tickets at craft fairs; hold bake sales, concerts, and raffles to raise additional money; and keep tuition costs to a minimum. An outer circle of barter has started within the group that provides goods and services needed to build each other's houses, harvest crops, and care for younger children.

Even colleges barter. Why do you suppose so many professors with teen-age children remain in posts with low pay scales? Because their children are eligible for free tuition at their colleges, or half tuition at other schools. George Washington University in Washington, D.C., has recognized educational benefits as a major factor in persuading employees to stay with them instead of taking more lucrative government jobs. In 1976 it was estimated that 1,330 students taking courses at GWU were attending through educational benefits given to employees. Not only children but employees and spouses as well are eligible for free or reduced-price courses (up to twelve free credit hours per calendar year for employees, half tuition for spouses). Security guards at universities instead of sleeping on the job are more likely to be studying; the job is a favorite post for graduate students. Other graduate students obtain use of equipment and labs in return for maintenance chores.

One early student at Harvard paid his tuition, according to the school's records, with "an old cow." The barter paid off handsomely when, in later years, he went on to become president of the university. Other schools, such as Goddard College in Plainfield, Vermont, allow students in the Adult Degree Program to use their jobs and family responsibilities as learning laboratories interspersed with brief residencies twice a year at the college, when past work is reviewed and a study plan for the upcoming six months formulated. Work/study programs at colleges like Northeastern University and the University of Cincinnati allow students to intersperse study with work in the field they wish to enter. Each job is filled by two students, who can earn enough to pay tuition.

Eckerd College, St. Petersburg, Florida, offered college tuitions through a local media broker for advertising credits. The broker was authorized to set up reciprocal arrangements in agreed-upon markets, providing scholarships for tuition valued at $2,500 per year in return for promotion and advertising. In the spring of 1974 a Philadelphia radio station offered three scholarships as prizes in a contest. Winners were required to meet admission standards, and arrangements for selection of the winners were made entirely by the radio station.

College educations are paid for by the government in return for military service or duty in the ROTC. Scholarships are available for students who promise to enter certain fields. Public and private schoolteachers taking student interns into their classes can get free courses from the intern's college. The teacher gets a double bonus: extra help in the classroom and free tuition. Ask at your college registrar's office who is eligible for free courses; see how you can fit into one of their descriptions.

Another way to barter for college costs is to become a resident assistant. In return for assuming responsibility for students (not as a disciplinarian), keeping an eye on the physical plant, organizing activities, fire drills, and counseling, you get a furnished room and tuition. Other students drive school buses for tuition or become managers of apartment complexes for free rent.

Retired executives donate their expertise to help others start businesses, or improve existing ones. Senior citizen groups teach classes in skills in return for the enjoyment of being active in the community and the opportunity of getting services.

Decide what you want to know, then find someone who teaches it or should be teaching it and ask how you can earn full or part tuition. Check professional magazines for educational opportunities available through conferences, seminars, and forums. Write a letter to the director inquiring what scholarships are available, enclosing a self-addressed, stamped envelope to facilitate his reply, as well as an outline of your qualifications as assistant director, registrar, librarian, or even standby speaker. If you have no marketable expertise, ask what jobs are available that the budget (perhaps stretched to the breaking point after paying the main speaker's fee) does not allow for that you can fill (such as waiting on tables).

If you are a writer, suggest that you come as a guest in search of article ideas that could become good promotion for the next event. Inquire well in advance of the time so that details can be worked out. If you don't receive an answer, write again after the director has had time to think over your offer; perhaps no one has suggested attending free before.

In 1975 David Milofsky won a waiter's scholarship to Middlebury College's Bread Loaf Writers' Conference; he attended the two-week workshop for only $100 instead of the full $400 tuition-and-board fee, waiting on table in the dining hall each mealtime in payment of the balance. The following year he became a Bread Loaf Scholar and attended free but paid $125 to offset costs of room and board, this time not waiting on tables. In 1977 he came full circle, as editor of *The Crumb,* the daily news sheet of the conference, when in addition to receiving free tuition, room, and board, he was paid $100, received a staff discount at the bookstore, and brought along his wife for a two-week vacation in the Vermont mountains.

David considers the original $100 fee the best investment he ever made. He is now well into his first novel, and each year's lectures improve the quality of his writing. He may (once the book has been published) return as a member of the winner's circle of best-selling authors for which Bread Loaf has become famous—an educational barter that could become a barter for fame.

Entertainment

Let Us Entertain You

One of the most outstanding entertainment barters on record happened years ago in the Society Islands when an opera singer from the Théâtre Lyrique de Paris received as her fee 3 pigs, 23 turkeys, 44 chickens (live), and 5,000 coconuts, not to mention "numerous bananas, lemons, and oranges." There is no record of what she said or sang at the sight of her remuneration, or that she booked passage home for her menagerie. Since the Society Islands did not have refrigeration at the time, one can only hope she had the good humor and imagination to stage an instant luau or barter her bounty for something less perishable, gaining in experience what she didn't receive in pay.

The Barter Colony in Abingdon, Virginia, which has been "eating" its box office since 1933, ran into similar surpluses during the Depression when culture-hungry patrons brought more berries, fruits, and vegetables than the actors and playwrights could digest or trade off. The management developed a distinct preference for cured country hams (one of which arrived on foot as late as 1973), and which may or may not be the origin of the term *ham actor*. Trades at the senior box office are mild compared with what has appeared at the Barter Playhouse for Children. What can you do with a toad and six marbles? Better yet, where can you trade them off for something you really need?

In the recent version of *King Kong*, the producer and Paramount Pictures gave Universal Studios 11 percent of their profits in return for Universal's canceling its own *King Kong* production plans. In 1976 Total Impact, Inc.—a group of enterprising actors who produced the movie *Getting Together*—bartered for half their expenditures, saving an estimated $75,000 to $125,000 in props, labor, and equipment. Living and working in a New York City studio whose rent was paid in exchange for services as building managers and superintendents, they may become the first janitors (if their efforts are successful) to win the Academy Award. With the cast and crew working for a percentage of the profits rather than cash, room and board had to be provided for as many as thirty people at one time. The cash came from commercial film work, delivering newspapers and selling Christmas trees, holding sidewalk sales and moving furniture. Having the only studio equipped to move a studio paid off handsomely with other barters: such as 500 gallons of paint to create a mural, 400 yards of carpet, a delicatessen to cater a wedding scene, ice cream for dessert. They now have, as a result of their bartering, a fully equipped film studio, a kitchen to produce cooking programs for TV, and a movie set in the director's home.

Free entertainment, available for barter, is everywhere, yours for the asking—whether singly, in couples, or as a group. What entertains you? What makes you happy? Name your fun, match the need of the source, fill it, and you too can be entertained for barter. If you are bashful and not accustomed to trading before an audience, try your hand at home entertainment.

Musicians need rooms in which to practice or instruments to play. If you can help them with their needs, they'll help you meet yours by performing at a children's party or the PTA. If they live in the city and you have a home in the country, invite them for weekends in return for entertaining at your parties.

Are you a drama buff? Call up the local theatrical group and ask if some of their actors or staff would like to come to your house for coffee or tea, if you provide a group of interested patrons as an audience for them to explain their work. Chances are they will come equipped with slides, movies, posters, or even passes, if you guarantee a number to make it worth their while. Or, check on nearby colleges, historical societies, restoration groups, and museums to see if they have a lecture bureau that will provide guest speakers, movies, or demonstrations for an audience. Try City Hall. There's not a politician alive who would turn down an opportunity to tell an audience his side of the story. If it's election year, ask your senator or representative.

Theatrical groups and touring companies have many needs for which they will barter free entertainment: costumes, transportation, storage, publicity, sewing, paint, tools, or printing, to name a few. College drama groups are always trading off performances with each other. When they travel abroad, they perform free in return for room and board along the way. What's good enough overseas is acceptable at home. Get a local organization to host visiting drama groups in return for free performances. Colleges will also trade services in return for speakers, orchestras, bands, choruses, concerts, or even circuses and conventions. City theater projects will perform free or accept admissions other than money. They will also stage benefits for worthy causes or needed trade-offs.

A shopping center in need of crowds will trade performing space to theatrical groups, giving free advertising for an event that will draw crowds. It's a good barter for a new group that needs public exposure.

Like to go to the theater? You don't have to pay money for tickets if you know where and how to get them. Everyone in that theater audience doesn't pay $10 for seats. Critics have their free seats on the aisle. Advertising people, newspapers, shopkeepers who promote the show in their windows, stores, or ads also receive free tickets. Theater people exchange seats to one another's shows.

You too can see the show free if you put your mind to it. Community theaters often hire ushers for one night of work in exchange for two seats at another performance. If you don't care to see the show again, swap them for tickets to another play, or give them to someone in return for something else.

If a theater is having problems filling up its seats, suggest to the manager that you pull together a group of patrons in exchange for a pair of free tickets. Or find someone who is unable to get to the theater alone and offer to drive or accompany him in return for a ticket. If you like "family" movies, find busy parents to pay for your ticket in return for taking their children along. It may become a habit.

Unless a show is sold out, it does no harm to the theater to give you a free ticket in exchange for a favor—your helping with props, answering the telephone, printing programs, addressing envelopes, or mending costumes saves them money and helps fill up the audience at the same time.

Set up a ticket exchange. Offer to sell or give away tickets for any show at the last minute so that when people are sick or have to work late, they will call you to unload them. (You, of course, can take some of the tickets in exchange for your services.) Any neighborhood could use a mechanism for swapping tickets. It can be newspaper classified ads ("Will swap two orchestra seats for *My Fair Lady* for equivalent tickets to Elton John concert"). Or try the radio, if the station has a free barter program. Set up a bulletin board at the supermarket or start a telephone chain among theater addicts. Sometimes, when everybody is busy or has seen a show, you will get tickets for nothing. If you have no use for them, barter for something you do want.

Suggest to a theater that it invite a senior citizen group as a tax deduction; offer yourself as an arranger—you will get free seats as the enabler or tour guide. Or be a source of ready information for theatrical needs in a community if you know where things are and how to get them—costumes, sets, mailing lists, and so on.

Whatever your form of entertainment, there is a way for you to barter for it. Like sailing? Help with the maintenance, be the crew, supply storage in winter months for the boat. Is playing tennis your form of entertainment? Paul Ridker brushes down his neighbor's tennis court each spring, keeping it in good condition, with the understanding that he can use it whenever it is available. A man who knows a good formula when he sees it, he now applies the same one with equal success to a neighbor's swimming pool.

Listening to records can be free, too. Greg Bryce has a used record and tape shop. He buys and sells. And he trades. If you bring him four used records worth $1 each, he will give you two $2.50 records, putting you both ahead. One accountant who regularly barters for his services wound up with a 5-foot stack of new records after a record store client went out of business.

If you can repair a stereo or television set, you are ahead of the game. A broken set may not be worth anything to its owner, who is usually glad to give it away. If it is not what you want but you are able to fix it, you can later trade it off for other things you need.

High school thespians will provide free modeling to stores in return for help with publicity for their productions. Golf courses will stage benefit events for worthy causes. Swimming and tennis clubs are always looking for ways to increase membership rolls. Find a way and be the means, and you may find yourself the recipient of a free membership.

We repeat: free entertainment, available for barter, is everywhere. What entertains you? Decide what you have to barter, and go out and get it. Then, let the world entertain *you.*

Fame

If You Want It, Flaunt It!

How far is up? How far is out? Who do you want to be? Where do you want to go? Who has to notice?

Fame means different things to different people. Some want to see their names in lights; others would be satisfied to have their neighbors recognize them. The secret to sure-footed success is to start small, think BIG, and be alert to possibilities around you.

The reason there are no statistics available on how many senators, movie stars, and celebrities bartered their way to fame (and sometimes fortune) is that barter is not as visible as money (unless a congressman affords it through appropriations). There are ways and there are ways. Which you use will depend on who you are, where you live, and where you want to go. Fame barters entail various combinations of time, talent, research, information, contacts, introductions, and daring. Here are a few.

Break a record. It doesn't have to be of Olympic quality to get your name in a record book but will take time, research, and imagination to choose the easiest route. It can seem as natural as baking the best pie in the county fair or as energetic as swimming the English Channel. Invent something that hasn't been done (such as building the world's smallest garage) or top an existing record (such as growing the longest fingernails or moustache, or shaking more than 8,513 hands in one day, or showering for more than seventy hours). If you are in business, make the biggest of whatever it is (chair, cake, or sign). Decide what you can do better than anyone else; decide who anyone else is; then start practicing. Make sure you alert the statistics keepers and the press before you take the final leap.

Meet a mass need. If someone had told you a few years ago that you could gain fame and make a fortune selling rocks as pets, you wouldn't have believed him, right? Or if, before that, someone had suggested drawing smiling faces on circles that said, "Have a happy day," you would have told him to climb back in his tree. But, using these examples, looking deep inside yourself to discover what needs you have that someone could fill, you may find a new craze and ride it to stardom. This kind of barter requires ingenuity, persistence, and a good agent.

Be a philanthropist. Give land or buildings to the community for a halfway house to be named after you. Give or loan something special to a museum and have it put your name on a card next to the object. Trade some of your stock to a college for a scholarship fund in your name. Andrew Carnegie did it with libraries. Maybe your community needs—a bus?

Get someone else to be a philanthropist, and be the middleman. Use his money, community land, a local organization, and then suggest the building be named after you.

Find something that has never been found before. This takes research, time, and luck. The Smithsonian's enormous collection of specimens was not all dug or netted by its staff. When amateur collectors send specimens to be identified and an institution like the Smithsonian has no such item in its collection, it will propose a deal. The first usually is on a par with a certificate (if that is what you are willing to accept). If you don't say yes right away, the institution may offer to put your name in print, someplace. Or, if you can practice restraint while barter chips are piled on the table, it may affix a little label announcing to the world that you collected that very insect. One man asked that his fossil be named after his wife (the Mrs. Smith Fossil?). Museums of any size operate on a shoestring and more often than not make barter a way of life. Fame (to whatever small degree) is their most abundant resource. Find out what your nearest museum doesn't have that it covets and provide it. Or . . .

Find the oldest, first, or most of something. An enterprising scientist in Minnesota found the oldest rockbed in captivity and is now selling it off for $6 a hunk. You may have the oldest state tree in your yard, or the greatest variety of ferns, or the first talking cat. Find it.

Be a pacesetter. Dare to stand out in a crowd. Once you have others following you, more people will ask your opinion and you'll gain a broader platform for your views. If your knowledge can match your guts, you'll be on your way. However, this route requires constant updating.

Start a new fad. Who'd have thought the hula hoop would become a craze? Or the yo-yo, or Silly Putty? Did you know that many toy designs are leased rather than sold? By bartering a percentage of temporary ownership to a toy company in return for production and marketing costs, an inventor can retain control of his creation, keeping the odds in his favor.

Write a best-seller. What do you know that others would like to learn? Put it in easy-to-understand language and you will have a how-to or an expo that others will pay to learn about.

Start a national controversy. If your name is Ellsberg and you have access to the Pentagon Papers, you have a head start, but think about it. You may come up with something.

Win a contest. This can be anything from a local bumper-sticker slogan to a national bake-off. Or, after a little research, you might find a funny tradition that you could practice and revive when you yourself have gained expertise (Pennsylvanians once held wheelbarrow races with blindfolded contestants).

Serve time (for a worthy cause, charity, or award committee). Provide a contrast to what the group already has. If everyone else is big on money, contribute personality.

Start an organization or a movement. You need only one member to start it—you. Lots of things have started this way: male libbers, the Marthas, the Good Sams, radio hams. Find a movement without an organization and create one. Barter for some stationery and start writing letters. One young friend of ours started a movement for a watershed and stopped the county commissioners dead in their tracks.

Give something unusual to a celebrity, and take along a photographer. Or . . .

Take something away from a celebrity and take along a photographer; but be careful what you take or you may end up with a lawsuit instead of fame.

Organize a one-man show of something. Andy Warhol made it

big with Campbell's Soup cans. No one has staked out a claim on mud pies or sand castles yet.

Get a company to sponsor publicity for your new interpretation of one of their products. Do a sculpture with Baggies and ask the manufacturer if it would be interested in giving you coast-to-coast publicity. If that fails, fill the bags with Jell-O and try selling the concept to General Foods. If that doesn't work, have a slumber party and invite the press. You may discover the most colorful (and tastiest) route to an orgy.

Write a letter to the president, pitched to evoke a response, and when it comes, publish it in the local newspaper.

Hang out where the élite meet. This takes a little class and dressing for the part, but it's easier to arrange than you might suppose. Keep up with gossip columns and the Celebrity Register, check out announcement boards in hotel lobbies, follow crowds on their way to a party. After you get the hang of it and learn how to get bounced with class, you can make a few contacts and be on your way (preferably in, not out).

Become involved in a love affair with a famous person. If Elizabeth Ray did it without an instruction book, so can you.

Form your own mob. A writer of our acquaintance has a barter dream that is cheap, easy, and of unlimited scope. It goes like this: Pick a group of people—ten in a small town, a hundred in a major city, more if the world is your gameboard. Select people of diverse talents and interests (the more influential the better) and strike a barter bargain. For one year you promote each other every time an opportunity presents itself. It works like a charm. Can't you imagine a friend of yours saying at a party, "The other day my friend Anders Holmquist said . . ."? Many of the listeners may never have heard of him, nor care who he is or what he said. But each time you mention his name, they will start wondering, Who the hell is Anders Holmquist? (Answer: He's the world's most sought-after flag and banner designer.) Another variation of this theme is to provide service free to each person who sends you five or ten additional clients; or a 5 percent discount for each additional client referred to you. As soon as you have enough backlog to pay the rent, cut out the practice and build up the receipts.

Give away something that everyone wants (or stake out a claim on a timely idea). Soon everyone will be coming to you for more. If you make great bread, start donating small amounts of it to good causes, build up a market, and before long you may have your own Pepperidge Farm.

If you can't think of anything to match bread, *find new ways of getting people to talk about you.* If that fails, talk about yourself to the right people. Dress designers, party givers, film stars, and realtors depend a great deal on word-of-mouth advertising and talk shows. If you are not so well known, sometimes the indirect approach is better. Seek out unrelated people who see media contacts on a regular basis. Get them to mention your name or idea every chance they get. Keep sources diversified so the target doesn't connect you with them.

Volunteer to do the grubby work in a high-power group (typing, addressing envelopes, passing out leaflets, licking stamps, putting up posters). It is one of the best ways to manage your way to the head of an organization.

Or, if you want to hit the public head on, *barter for a billboard.* Put up anything you want that makes you feel good. How about: "Congratulations, Birch Hotz. You're terrific!" Sit back and watch the fireworks.

Be best at something. Unlike record breaking (a one-shot deal after years of practice) or meeting a mass need (which takes a certain amount of masterful planning), being the best of what you already are may be the best route to fame. Even if you never find the pot of gold, the rainbow will fill your life, you will have the satisfaction of having done your best, and you will attract friends who are just right for you.

Farming

The Grass Just May Be Greener
...or Is That Money?

Barter has been a way of life with American farmers since the Pilgrims first landed on Plymouth Rock. The cornerstone for social events such as barn-raising, quilting bees, and love feasts (held at churches in spring and fall), barter was also used to clear, till, and harvest the land, and to build houses.

Farmers made everything in early days from the clothes on their backs to the tools in their hands. As historians count the number of tools (boxes, bowls, baskets, crocks, drainers, strainers, measures, weights, yokes, totes, straps, traps, and jacks, to name a few), they wonder how pioneers found the time to fill them, much less make them.

When farmers went to town or market they took along surplus to trade for what they needed. Before long, it was obvious which family made the best crocks, the strongest baskets, and the most efficient wagons. Individuals discovered that if they made additional numbers of what they made well, their efforts counted double in trades, and if signed or marked, more again.

In time, many farmers became tradesmen in town, and because barter had become a way of life (since money was not always that plentiful or dependable), they continued the practice. The miller ground wheat in return for a percentage of the crop; the blacksmith took payment in food or services. Until World War II many general stores, hardwares, and even undertakers took all or part payment in barter.

Today, although larger farms and combines deal strictly for

cash, many small farmers as well as transplanted professionals from the city pursue barter as one of the blessings of country life. One author, who lives on a large farm with many buildings and has neither the time nor the talent for chores, sharecrops his fields for one-third of the crop (or half if the farmer uses his barn for storage). Hunters get permission to hunt if they share their bounty of meat or pheasant feathers. Trappers keep muskrats and beavers out of his pond in return for pelts. The fifty or sixty chickens he raises annually are killed, plucked, and frozen by a neighbor who keeps one of each ten she processes. His pigs are butchered by a farmer in exchange for the pannhouse and pudding (porridge made from leftover parts). His woods are thinned regularly by another neighbor who cuts timbers into fireplace logs, leaving him half. He often trades off country hams for maintenance jobs such as insulating the attic.

Large farms hire tenant farmers, who receive free housing, telephone, utilities, half a beef a year, sometimes a car or truck, and up to $150 a week pay—how much depending on how well the tenant barters when he is hired. Other farmers barter use of machinery for a portion of another farmer's crop or help in harvesting their own. (In trading services for equipment, farmers equate in man-days. A tractor used one day is worth one man-day; a thresher, two man-days; while smaller items like mowers are worth a half.) Or two farmers who live near each other each buy half the equipment needed and use it jointly all the time. Many farmers don't trade in older pieces of equipment they no longer use, preferring to keep them as barter to trade off on other equipment, either on a one-shot deal or over a period of years, sometimes leasing it on a regular basis in return for labor or shares. Some work out permanent deals, renegotiable on a year-to-year basis, threshing crops in return for making silage, or (in the case of clover) selecting every fifth bushel of seed before the rest is gathered up.

Cow pools barter milk and cream in return for refrigerated truck services to take it to the processing plant. Use of land is swapped for manure fertilizer. Bedding costs of animals are bartered for veterinarian services or artificial insemination of cattle. Farms with natural outgrowths of watercress give wholesalers access for picking in return for doing city errands or a percentage of profits or pickings. Tree farmers trade grafting and seedlings to nurseries in return for landscaping around the house.

If a farmer wants a pond built for fire protection or watering animals, he can have designs and specifications drawn up free by the federal soil conservation agency in return for his promise to follow them. He can then get the ASCS to pay half the cost if he agrees to follow the plans. The wildlife commission will stock the pond with fish if he allows a limited amount of public fishing; and he can obtain free seedlings from the state forestry in return for his promise not to go into the Christmas tree business or remove trees by the roots to thin out growth. (It's all right to cut them down at Christmas time and sell them, but not on a large scale.)

Fruit orchards often allow pickers to keep 2 bushels for each 10 they pick for the owner. Large fruit growers allow hunters the use of buildings for migrant workers in return for maintenance. Wool from sheep is traded for yarn or finished material.

On the more sophisticated side, many landowners raise everything from oysters to bees to gain tax benefits; others keep them unprofitable for as many years as possible to offset other profits. One doctor, who bought several hundred acres as an investment and tax deduction, started raising horses as a hobby loss and hit a winner both in horses and life-style when he discovered that he had to show a profit for only two out of seven years. He used profits to hire a trainer, improve the strain, buy machinery and trailers, build a pond and stables, and travel all over the United States attending horse shows and inspecting prospective purchases. When his hobby became excessively lucrative, he gave up his medical practice to indulge it full-time, but after he lucked into a few champions, he had to reopen his office to balance his profits with expenses.

One-horse owners who have difficulty keeping up with the high cost of feed have discovered another form of bartering in farm life—gleaning. Modern machinery used for harvesting does not gather up what falls to the ground. Consequently, horse owners have in recent years gotten into the habit of keeping a watch on nearby fields to be first to pick up the leavings. If they don't first ask for permission, they can be arrested for trespassing. However, if they do ask (and especially if they get advance permission), the farmer is only too glad to grant it—in return for one-half or one-third of what they find.

If you notice a busy farmer who doesn't have time to reap the harvest from his nut trees, offer to do the job for halves.

The award for the best business-and-pleasure barter in farming must go to the farmer who wanted to take his wife on vacation and leave the children at home. His solution? A young childless couple down the road came up with the perfect trade: two weeks of twenty-four-hour baby- and housesitting in return for half a cow—butchered and wrapped, of course.

Food

Developing a Taste for Barter

Food is nearly as universal a barter medium as money. Since it is a basic and constant need of human life, no barter mechanism has greater potential for finding a trade.

Little Tommy Tucker sang for his supper. In the nursery rhyme about the Old Woman and Her Pig, a handful of hay was traded for a saucer of milk.

If you have food to trade, find someone who is hungry. If you are hungry, find someone who has excess food, or supplies in danger of spoiling; a profitable deal is inevitable. During the Depression a Minneapolis barter organization considered sauerkraut the gold reserve of its system.

Peru has a form of silent barter: one person makes a little pile of potatoes; the other counters with a pile of squash. Each then adds or subtracts as the negotiations continue, until the barter is finalized. Jurgen Haber bartered his way through Peru in 1972. Traveling with a truckful of things he didn't need, he supported himself on his "trash," trading old tennis shoes, empty plastic milk bottles (without tops for one orange; with tops, two oranges). Although he never found language a barrier, he admits to consuming a great deal of fruit on the trip.

Home gardeners quickly learn the Zucchini Rule of Barter: during planting time, no one wants to throw away half a packet of seeds; but after harvest, with the freezer full and stomachs overflowing from zucchini casserole and zucchini cake (not to mention zucchini soup), almost anything looks like a good trade. The Zucchini Rule applies to fishermen and foragers as well. Find anyone who grows, catches, hunts, or gathers food, and acquire a taste for his excess. Trade your bumper crop of potatoes for your neighbor's leeks and you both profit with vichyssoise. Or help with weeding for "shares." Trade raw ingredients for cooked or preserved foods, or barter produce for household services, maintenance, or even transportation of a crop to market. Harvest your neighbor's cherries in exchange for the stemless ones; his peaches for the misshapen ones. During periods of overabundance, cook twice as much for dinner and invite the neighbors. You'll be invited back (if you ask the right ones) and it could become a weekly attraction, giving you a night off once a week at no expense to your budget. Or, if you have a large lot, divide it into sections and let yardless friends farm free in return for part of their crop.

When *Mother Earth News* called for barter stories, the response confirmed the success of food barters. One person traded his honey to farmers who allowed him to set hives on their land. Another exchanged eggs and sprouts for weekly laundering. A fisherman found a way to vary his diet by bartering with a hunter. A strawberry crop was shared in exchange for freezer space, dandelion wine for electrical repairs. One woman grew walnuts specifically as a barter crop; another traded half her crop of olives for lessons in how to cure them. In barter fairs, which are gaining in popularity across the country, maple syrup trades faster than any other crop. If you have a neighbor who raises food, find out what his needs are. You may be able to get pickles for jars or vegetables for a supply of paper bags; or he may rake your lawn to add to his compost pile.

Kent Whealy (c/o Charlie M. Cunningham, RR 2, Princeton,

Missouri 64673) started the True Seed Exchange, which swaps
seed coast-to-coast, usually heirloom tried-and-true strains no
longer available in stores.

You can also trade crop for crop, as fishermen do with farmers.
Maine lobstermen used to throw back excess until they realized
farming neighbors were only too happy to barter fruits and vegetables in exchange for fruits of the sea. Food barters can also involve
information exchanges: an older, more experienced farmer advising another in return for help with his crop, or telling someone
where your secret mushroom-hunting spot is in exchange for a
cache of wild raspberries or persimmons. This can grow to finding
a contact in Indiana for pawpaws, an Oregonian for Comice pears,
or a Vermont source for maple syrup. It not only balances your diet
without cost, but often procures delicacies money can't buy.

If you have no food to trade, help in processing a crop, or ask a
grower if you can keep a share of what you pick (see Farming).
Fishermen trade extras for a quart of the chowder, or for help with
maintenance of their boat. Oranges for marmalade, grapes for
wine, or even grapes for winemaking lessons—rich barters are
there for the picking. On large farms where machines harvest the
crop, much is left lying on the ground. Ask the farmer if you can
pick it up by hand in return for shares (again with half or a third
going to him).

If your wheat is infested with bugs, trade it to a chicken farmer
as feed in exchange for (naturally) chickens. Country doctors and
lawyers often accept produce as payment during harvest season. If
you have an unused room in your house and let the local food cooperative group use it as a store, you can usually get your supplies
free or at a 50 percent discount. Many co-ops give a 20 percent discount on a month-to-month basis (your card gets stamped when
you fulfill the requirements) in return for four hours of work. If
you don't put in your required hours or services (like making runs
to the warehouse), you pay 25 percent above cost.

If you have extra land, rent it to a local farmer for one-third or
one-half of the crop. Or fence it in and raise your own meat. Raise
extra meat to trade for other food or help with the butchering.
Help someone else with his butchering in return for a portion of
the meat.

If you live in a city, there are opportunities to receive your food already cooked in return for helping in hospitals and homes for the aged, or delivering meals to shut-ins. One retired man, an insomniac, took advantage of his ailment by arranging a barter with a group of local merchants. He now patrols the streets nightly checking the shops in return for free meals during the daytime at various restaurants, with the group paying the tab.

In colonial days butter and tobacco were as good as money. A potter often received his pay for making whiskey jugs for the local distillery in (you guessed it) whiskey. As such things tend to do, the tradition has grown into an institution. In 1975 Kettle River, Idaho, hosted several hundred people for a two-day barter and harvest festival, which started out as a trading post for simple garden produce. Everything from tools to massages was exchanged. People bartered everything from the trucks they drove to the clothes they wore; they even swapped stories and songs.

On a local level, get your church to sponsor a God's acre sale, or check with the state economic and development section or conservation departments to find out what free advice, free seeds or trees to plant, ponds, or fish are available. Read up on wild food so that day trips pay off with produce. Save unused coupons and trade them for those you want. Refund Reports (818 Bridge St., Ellwood City, Pennsylvania 16117) will send you a sample newsletter for 35¢ or a three-month trial subscription for $1, or keep you on their mailing list for a year for $3. Refund Round-Up (401 Newton Ave., Oaklyn, New Jersey 06107) sends a sample for 35¢ and a three-month subscription for $1.65. Refund Blank Exchange (Box 122, Sandwich, Massachusetts 02463) will send you thirty coupons in return for thirty you don't want if you enclose 25¢ and a self-addressed stamped envelope.

Many local groceries can't afford paid help but will let you work off your bill by waiting on counter, taking inventory, or storesitting while the owners go on vacation.

Become friends with a restaurant critic; they always need company on their tours, or you can provide them with information and/or favors in return for an occasional meal.

Or be a critic. Many small-town weeklies or smaller urban newspapers pay critics with meals on the town for two.

When a new food shop or restaurant opens near you, stop by and see what they need that you no longer want. One Washington antique dealer, Sue Jones, gained 10 pounds on a barter when she sold an old scale to the Booeymonger delicatessen for meal credits. Any food faddist whose fancies outpace his pocketbook can do the same. The answer to whetting your appetite may be just around the corner . . . or in your own backyard.

Furnishings

Doing the Digs Through Barter

One of the world's famous pictures, Paul Revere's portrait by John Singleton Copley, was painted in payment of the bill Copley owed Revere for silver. Early furniture stores doubled as funeral parlors, one business feeding the other in slow months. Almost anything was accepted as payment for furniture or funerals—materials for caskets, wood for both businesses, gravedigging for furniture.

Without realizing it, many furniture dealers have a built-in acceptance for barter. Sometimes all it takes is a gentle reminder. There are many ways to acquire furniture through barter, depending on whether you like to pick it up or prefer to have it delivered to your door.

Some methods are clean; others are dirty. If you use furnishings in your business (as a product consultant or interior decorator, for example) and have access to samples, you can test items before you sell them to someone else; or let people visit your place on their way to new homes. You can bargain with developers to work as nightwatchman protecting model homes without pay in return for selecting X amount of furniture for X months of work. Some developers prefer to "open-list" houses with several realtors rather than give exclusives and consequently must hire demonstrators to show casual browsers through on weekends as well as keep an eye on the merchandise. Other builders work out deals with cleaning persons, paying them with furnishings instead of money; or they let unlicensed salespersons collect their percentage of sales in furnishings. In dealings of this nature, be sure the developer is actually the owner and not a hireling; and get the agreement in writing to protect yourself. Otherwise, you may discover you have accepted stolen merchandise for time you could have invested in more profitable undertakings.

Some furniture stores allow credit to realtors who send them lucrative orders and/or new customers. If you are a shopowner, teacher, or Welcome Wagon lady, you may be eligible for the same fringe benefits. One-man shops trade merchandise for regular chores (cleaning, refinishing damaged pieces, advertising, printing, sign painting, clerical help, inventory keeping, window decorating, driving, storesitting). Others, in need of additional space, will trade credit for storage.

Realtors with little time often find themselves in a bind when the former owner moves out leaving a mess and the new resident is waiting to move in. If the house has not been sold, a realtor is even more anxious to have it cleaned so that he can start showing it to prospective buyers. Strike a bargain when his need is greatest. Offer to clean up properties at a reduced rate in return for keeping all leftovers, which can be items too heavy to move (such as pianos) or discards that are easily traded to someone else.

If you own a truck, loan it to friends for moving in return for furniture, or for first tabs on what they leave behind. Start a service cleaning out attics, basements, garages, or barns with the agreement that you can keep or sell off all throwaways; take unwanteds to flea markets to trade for what you want. Trade wood pieces and parts to a restorer in return for work on your furniture or for a piece he doesn't have time to do. Apprentice yourself to a furniture refinisher for furniture instead of pay. Offer to help an antique dealer recane chairs or repair furniture in return for merchandise of items "in the rough" he no longer wants.

If you are expert enough, volunteer free antique appraisals to friends in return for an item from their collections. Help an auctioneer list a sale, or help the family on sale day, in return for selecting what you want from the house contents. Check out the local upholsterer. More often than not he has excess pieces clogging up his inventory uncollected by owners that he will sell cheaply to gain the space or trade for help. If you decide on the latter route and learn how to upholster, you have another skill to trade. You can then upholster someone else's chair in return for their buying you the material for yours.

Help price items in a tag or garage sale in exchange for your choice of merchandise, or manage the sale for a percentage of the profit (paid in furnishings, of course).

If you are skilled in cabinetry, offer to make a piece of furniture for a friend in return for his buying the lumber for yours. If you have standing timber on your land, trade it to the local lumberyard on "halves," getting 50 percent of it back "dressed" to make into furniture or trade off to someone who can.

Volunteer to price for a bazaar committee so that you can get first choice on specials. If you are able to buy more bargains at the sale, resell them at a profit. You may break even, getting what you bought free.

Many elderly and divorced persons exchange furniture for services, preferring to hang on to their cash for groceries. Some art galleries have barter corners where art is available for barter. If your community gallery doesn't have one, suggest it. When New York–based artist Miriam Schapiro offered to trade paintings at her one-woman show in Chicago, she listed what she would like to receive in return. By the end of the show she had bartered paintings and collages for Persian rugs, a quilt, architectural services, materials, and a vacation home in France and at last report was angling for two air conditioners.

Other artists pay for services, rent, frames, and materials with art. One country artist, after being turned down by the local gallery, volunteered to hang her works in the neighborhood hardware store for a percentage of any they sold. They not only outdid the local gallery in sales but became so attached to her landscapes that they offered to barter merchandise credits for full value of her price tags.

Houses slated for demolition are lucrative sources of furniture. When the occupants move out they take what they want, leaving much behind. Ask the supervisor for permission to haul out what you want. Built-ins from other eras, such as three-sided corner cupboards, can be removed and rebuilt into new rooms or stand alone with new backs as single pieces. Shutters, once standard equipment in Victorian homes, make great replacements for curtains, don't have to be ironed, and don't even have to fit the windows. They can be free-standing on sills, moving on when you do. Spindles from broken stairways can be reinstalled as space dividers or redesigned as towel racks. Old shelving (often chestnut or mahogany) can be recycled into tables, benches, frames, TV cabinets, and desks.

Some of the best finds in furniture, according to one antique dealer, are discovered along country roads where they have been pitched to save trips to the dump. It's a joke in the antique trade, when a dealer doesn't have something in stock, to say he's going to check his "warehouse" (meaning the town dump). Dumps are treasure houses of antiques: old ice chests that can be made into bars; refrigerators that can be converted to meat and fish smokers; old washing machines with copper linings that can double as wood containers next to a fireplace or decorator planters for indoor trees. Dumps are marvelous resources for offbeat props, which can be bartered to window designers or theatrical companies as background devices.

One scavenger (or scrounger, as we say in the trade) suggests making the rounds an hour ahead of pickup trucks on trash collection nights. "Wear gloves," he advises, "if you are wary of germs; and if you're well known, a face mask." If you are leery of such after-dark activity, make friends with those who enjoy the thrill of the chase so you can be first on their list for bests.

Professional moving companies sometimes give away or trade off damaged furniture after the insurance company has replaced it with new. Those with storage facilities hold annual auctions of unclaimed furniture or sell off items whose storage bills have not been paid. Check local movers to see if they would be interested in trading off has-beens in return for nightwatchman or clerical duties, or preparing for the next auction. Other auctioneers, if they don't get a high enough opening bid for an item, bypass it, leaving it free for the asking. Be first to ask.

Organizations and foundations that can't afford to buy up complete collections at auction often work out reciprocal deals with an owner, guaranteeing him lifetime occupancy in return for donating the collection to them. Many historical houses are furnished with items on permanent loan from owners who prefer their rarities to be housed in a protected environment. Other owners of loaned items forget to come after them, making them permanent acquisitions of house museums. State historical societies will trade lifetime occupancy in historic houses in return for the occupant's collection of furnishings and/or help with the interior restoration.

Spread the word. Let people know you want free furniture. Before long, you may receive a phone call in the middle of the night from someone you don't even know saying, "It's yours. Come pick it up." With enough of the right kind of thinking, it may even deliver itself to your house.

Gifts

Gifted Ideas

The best gifts are not in the store—they are in your hands, your heart, your mind, your skills. Gift barters require time, experience, imagination, and friendship. They are the most difficult to realize but the longest remembered.

First is the gift of self. What do you do that others enjoy or envy? If the recipient likes your home, invite him to a small gathering in his honor. Your garden? Take him a basket of flowers or vegetables. Give him a written promise as elaborate or as simple as you please: ten back rubs, five manicures, ten long walks in the country, a week's camping, six car washings, a brainstorming to solve a problem, or new customers for his business.

If you dare, and truly trust the friendship, suggest that each year you select one thing from the other's home to keep as your very own. Two friends who have been doing this for over ten years report great surprise at what the other covets, only one refusal, and absolutely no overindulgences.

If your friend makes wine, save up your bottles for a year. If he's restoring his house, find that missing ingredient he needs and has not been able to find, or duplicate a part of your house that he envies. Find a part to something else, like the tray under a candle snuffer, or your pieces of a friend's china pattern.

How about a temporary loan of something she'd never dare ask for? Like your favorite dress for a special occasion, your car for transportation, your mink coat to take on vacation? And don't forget your children for company (a gift especially appreciated after a death in the family).

Possibilities, once you put your mind to bartering for gifts, are limitless. A surprise party? A new experience—going to a mineral spring, having a massage, picking mushrooms? Sharing a friend, introducing him to a celebrity or someone in his field that he has always wanted to meet? Find a contact, or better yet, a contract, for a consultant friend. Put your talents at his disposal to use in any way he wishes; or, if you lack in this department, work out a barter deal with your neighborhood craftsman and let your friend select from his wares. Trade your brownies for a bottle of wine, your old frames for a dried-flower arrangement, or address envelopes for a local organization to pay for a friend's membership.

Find out what his needs are and barter to meet them. Maybe it's plowing once a year, or weeding during summer months, or raking leaves in the fall. For an older person who is confined to her house, bring the world to her doorstep. Barter with a local drama group to put on a play in her honor (see Entertainment). Do a favor for a local author to get an autographed book to give for a present, or with an art student for a watercolor of a friend's house.

If you travel a great deal, use your contacts to fill your friends' shopping lists. Keep a special place for trade-off barter presents—things too good to give away, too special to sell. Or, for the person who has everything, give a box of wishes, one for every day of the month or year.

Barter gifts reseed themselves, grow in any climate, and are usually returned with interest. The next time you need a gift, don't look in the store. Go shopping in your heart.

Hobbies

Anyone for Hobbies?

"Every man has two educations: one which he receives from others, and one, more important, which he gives to himself."

—EDWARD GIBBON

Do you remember your first hobby? Is it rooted in your present occupation? Has it become the golden thread of your existence, weaving your work and life together so that you can't tell where one ends and the other begins? Do you wish it did? Or does your passion for your hobby lie in the deepest recesses of your mind, ready to explode into action at some future date?

Young matchbook collectors have a way of growing into world travelers and travel agents. Beer can collectors can't resist dumps (in the form of landfill or bars). College girls who collect fraternity pins seem to do the same with husbands. And nine times out of ten, a computer specialist hooked on seed catalogs is a frustrated would-be farmer.

Hobbies thrive when they are shared with kindred spirits. They develop wider scope, greater meaning, and dynamism in the mutual sharing of admiration and cooperation. Often the only way to obtain the choicest information, items, or materials necessary to indulge your passion is through barter or exchange. Other collectors will not let go of their choicest, scarcest, and most expensive things unless you can guarantee them something of equal value and quality they want more. This is only one of the reasons hobbies have a way of growing into clubs, organizations, publications, and before you know it, a movement (like the CBers).

A hobby is any occupation, activity, or interest (stamps, gardening, sewing), primarily pleasurable, that one pursues. As Honoré de Balzac so aptly put it, "A man who has no hobby does not know the good that is to be drawn out of life. A hobby is a happy medium between a passion and a monomania." But the power and opportunity to improve your hobby lie in direct proportion to the number of contacts made. Therefore, to get in the running:

Join a club. Kindred spirits have duplicates, extras, and also information on where the best things are, as well as what triggers the weakness of the present owner (good ammunition in any trade). As a club you can form a cooperative to buy supplies at a discount and may be eligible for group discounts on magazines; or take subscriptions to separate magazines for each other (the rate on gifts may be lower), trading off with each other every month so everyone has an opportunity to read them all (see Books, Magazines, and Newspapers; and Organizations). You can barter with top collectors to lecture to your group in return for honorariums, which can be a present for their hobby rather than money. You can also run a group ad in the local paper or one of the many hobby magazines to find more sources of supply. You will learn of other clubs nationwide specializing in the same field with whom you can trade items or information, be invited to their swap fests, and by affiliation get on more mailing lists.

Take out a subscription to magazines or newspapers specializing in your hobby. There are all kinds of publications geared to special interests. For example, the *Horseless Carriage Gazette* (bimonthly, $8; 9031 E. Florence Avenue, Downey, California 90240); *Muzzle Blasts* ($8; P.O. Box 67, Friendship, Indiana 47021); *Silver* (bi-monthly, $7; 1619-A S.W. Jefferson Street, Portland, Oregon 97201); or *Americana,* which covers many hobbies (10 Rockefeller Plaza, New York, New York 10020). (See Books, Magazines, and Newspapers on how to barter for a subscription.) Check out the ads—what you are looking for may be waiting on its pages. Keep back issues for information on prices and markets for ready reference.

Advertise. Take an ad in one of the publications catering to hobbyists such as *Hobbies* ($6 a year; 1006 South Michigan Ave.,

Chicago, Illinois 60605), which specializes in glass, china, dolls, and coins; or *Antique Trader* (published weekly for $9.50 a year; P.O. Box 1050, Dubuque, Iowa 52001), which contains 70 percent advertising. Or try the swap column in *Yankee* Magazine (Dublin, New Hampshire 03444).

Frequent flea markets. As you become a regular, sellers will call you as soon as they find something new. Trade for it, using your extras or duplicates. Most flea marketeers prefer trading for cash because they think with their expertise they will get the better deal.

Specialize in something hobbyists in your field can't find anyplace else so you'll be first in line for specials. If you collect dolls, learn how to repair them; trade repairs for more parts. Once you build up your supply, dolls will come to you, and as you gain a monopoly, you can trade for anything you want. If you collect buttons, invent an ingenious display case and you will soon have the names and addresses (on orders for same) of all the buttoneers with specimens stashed away in jars and closets.

Accept what you don't need to trade off at a future date. Mechanical banks have become so scarce that clubs won't divulge their membership list or accept you as a member until they contact you by phone and check out your collection in person. (A good bank collection can run over $1 million, so collectors can't be too cautious.) New members are advised never to sell extras, but to use them as trade; and whenever they see a "still" going at a good price, to snap it up to barter for mechanicals they don't have. The greatest trading power in obtaining mechanical banks is not money but more banks.

Become an appraiser. If your hobby involves things (rather than activities) and you are a registered appraiser (which insurance companies require for reimbursement purposes), you can charge by the hour or on a percentage basis—but who says you have to be paid money?

Post notices on swap or bulletin boards at grocery stores, laundromats, hobby and craft shops, listing what you are interested in trading.

Go to the source of supply. If you know the town where an item was originally manufactured, auctions and sales there will provide a larger percentage of what you're looking for. You will also find out more information on your subject. Advertise in the local newspaper for what you don't find.

Become an expert. The only difference between a collector and an expert is that an expert organizes his materials and takes slides. As you read books, go to museums, and research your subject, your contacts as well as your knowledge will expand. You can trade information for additional information or more objects and supplies. If you write articles for hobby publications (they may pay you in copies or subscriptions, but that's all right), you will be the person others seek for trades or opinions. You will become sought after as a speaker, and instead of money you can accept honorariums of choice items for your collection.

A hobby has a way of taking over your life, but the time involved and the results it produces could easily become the most treasured legacy you leave to your children.

"No man is really happy or safe without a hobby," Sir William Osler once said, "and it makes precious little difference what the outside interest may be . . . botany, beetles, or butterflies, roses, tulips or irises, fishing, mountaineering or antiquities . . . anything will do so long as he straddles a hobby and rides it hard."

Happy riding!

Housekeeping

"Housekeeper: *n.* one who has charge of domestic tasks in a household."
—*The American Heritage Dictionary of the English Language*

The problem with bartering in housekeeping, as Snow White discovered when she ran away from her wicked stepmother to the house of the seven dwarfs, is determining who is in charge. Who sets the ground rules on hours and buying apples from door-to-door salesmen? The person in charge of the house or the one in charge of the work?

Houseowners are often so glad to have help with the chores that they forget to ask questions, much less take time to find answers. Housekeeping means different things to different people. On one end of the scale you have the "Cleanliness is next to godliness" crowd, while others are content to have a path cleared to the sink. Separately there's no problem, but if they end up in the same pad like the Odd Couple, friction is bound to result.

Therefore, if you have a house that needs keeping and you think bartering is the answer, ask yourself some questions before you start interviewing: Are you looking for full- or part-time help? Temporary or permanent? Does it matter what time of the day or night work is done? Could it be accomplished on weekends? Do you want live-in or day help? Does the age, sex, or marital status of the applicant matter? Do you mind children being around during the day? Is the work heavy or light? Does it involve additional things like cooking or telephone answering? Are there children or elderly persons in your family to care for?

Is your house large or small? Each has its advantages and problems. A large house may look like more work, but if it has extra room for a live-in, it could be an advantage. A good address is a plus because you will have to trade less to get a barter. A small house might mean less work but could present personality problems for live-ins. Is your house close enough to town so that a housekeeper can go without a car, or are you providing one for errands? Can it be used for other things, without permission each time?

Next, what kind of person are you—easy to get along with or fussy? Do you like things cleaned instantly or is once a week enough? Do you like everything out of sight and in order? Or don't you care as long as dinner gets on the table? Does anything gritty underfoot make your teeth itch? Are you willing to share the work to get it done? What else are you willing to share—your family? Sometimes the only reason someone takes on the job is to become a member of a family. What's your noise tolerance? Does it bug you to hear a loud radio or TV while the work is being done?

What other fringe benefits can you offer: separate living arrangements; an apartment? The more you can add to this side of the balance sheet, the choosier you can be in the selection. May a housekeeper entertain guests? And with your things, or must she use only her room or apartment? Set priorities before you start interviewing so you will know the questions to ask and not find yourself living with someone else's answers.

If you represent an organization searching for help with a church, clubhouse, or historic building in return for quarters, what kind of checks and balances do you have to guarantee controlling problems? What are the duties? Who can be admitted during off-hours? Is the housekeeper allowed to use all the building or only private quarters?

Where to look. If you have a piano and live near a conservatory or music academy, students may be willing to trade housekeeping duties for living accommodations that include a piano. Or if you live near a neighborhood bar, perhaps its pianist might enjoy sharing your housework to live within walking distance of his job. If you work days and he works nights, other problems would also be solved.

Advertise in the paper under Wanted, Employment, or Help Wanted. Look in the paper under Situations Wanted or Personal Services. Give someone an idea he hasn't thought of by advertising where he would be looking for a job or home, such as Apartments for Rent, Rentals, Help Wanted, or Rooms. "Will trade free room and board in return for light housekeeping" (or whatever the conditions are), followed by your telephone number, will bring applicants; or if you prefer anonymity, list a box number for written replies. Post notices on bulletin boards at grocery stores. Check columns in *Yankee* Magazine (Dublin, New Hampshire 03444) and *Mother Earth News* (P.O. Box 70, Hendersonville, North Carolina 28739).

If your living accommodations include a studio or garage ideal for a fledgling business, call local groups in that field (such as craftsmen's organizations) and advertise in trade publications. Check senior citizen clubs. If you have young children, you may be blessed with a housekeeper and substitute grandparent in the same person.

Call the personnel or housing director of the nearest large company or factory, describing what kind of work you have and what you are willing to trade. If any of the employees are looking for a place to live, or simultaneously trying to swing night school and car payments, he may know where to find them. If the person is on the nightshift, he can housekeep during the day while you are at work. If he works days and studies at night, perhaps the work can be done on weekends.

Colleges are always looking for rooms for students, and many students after paying tuition have little left for rent. Call the housing office at the college, or the director for residential living, who will post your notice on the bulletin board, put it in the college newspaper, or, if you prefer, keep the information on file in the office.

Call local churches, volunteer fire companies, and fraternal organizations. If you live in the city, advertise in a country newspaper. If your residence is in the country, advertise in city newspapers for someone who wants a change of scene.

Check the nearest embassy. Foreign students and new immigrants often need a place to stay or a sponsor for the first year in order to get a visa. If you can speak a foreign language, check language departments of nearby institutions for students already here who need fluency in English.

If you think you could settle for temporary help and know a craft or skill that others want to learn (upholstering, pottery, macramé), offer to trade lessons in return for getting your work done. If you have teaching skills, try tutoring for housekeeping barters.

Do you live near a hospital? Call the nursing office supervisor. Sometimes a parent who wants to stay near a sick child can't afford a private room with extra bed or the added expense of staying in a motel. If the hospital doesn't already arrange housing, suggest that it start or offer to find a volunteer group to coordinate it.

Want exciting company around the house? Check out professional theaters and leave a standing offer: free room and board in return for light housekeeping or chores. Many theaters have intern programs whose students, after buying tickets to the big city, can't afford rent. If they have difficulty talking their parents into letting them trip the light fantastic, sharing a private home might give them the permission they need. Other theaters need rooms on a regular basis for actors working for minimum scale.

Call the state employment service in your town (listed in the telephone book under the name of your state). It handles barter arrangements as well as paid jobs and will take your order, put it on file, and try to sell it to those in need of a job. Check out-of-town relatives to see if any cousins want to attend school in your city, or need a place to spend the summer in return for a little work.

How great a risk are you willing to take? If you feel equipped to help someone with a problem and are willing to make the personal investment, get in touch with your local high school counselor and offer your home to a student who has family problems (sometimes the delinquent is the parent and not the child). It may require additional supervision on your part and you may have to get permission from the parent if the child stays at your house for more than twenty-four hours, but helping a young person find new hope could make you happier than an ultraclean house.

Homes for unwed mothers often need places for young women during pregnancy, admitting them only when they reach full term. But again, such a lodger may have personal problems and decisions to work out. Are you willing to get involved?

Residents of "old folks" homes are not always that elderly and are there because they have no place else to go. Some are free to leave during the day and need only transportation. If healthy, they might prefer to live at your house and free their bed for someone who needs it more. Call the director or chaplain of the nearest facility to inquire.

Local mental health departments need havens for women leaving their husbands who require a home until they develop the skills to earn their living. They may have emotional problems and children, but sometimes a home away from the battle zone and a regular routine may be better medicine than any the doctor can prescribe.

Mental health organizations need placements for people under treatment for alcohol, drug, or emotional problems. Housekeeping for someone who cares could help them to break past patterns.

Call Social Services (usually listed in the telephone book under the city or county in which you live) and ask for a social worker. Outline what you need done and they will try to match your job to someone in their files. Older people without children are easier to place but sometimes can't handle heavy work; younger people who can do heavy work often have problems (such as alcohol or drugs) or have children to care for. Spell out everything in advance and make sure the person is in good health. When runaways are placed in a foster home through such agencies, they are not expected to do any more housework than other children in the family.

Parolees who have served time sometimes cannot leave an institution because they can't find living arrangements. If you are willing to provide a home for one in trade for doing the housework, contact the parole officers or clergy at institutions near you, or "outreach" groups in local churches. At smaller institutions such as the county jail, ask for the warden or counselor. However, if you are an elderly gentleman searching for a "young lady housekeeper," be prepared to provide references and pay at least $25 weekly, as parole officers usually advise women to ask for "getting away" money in such arrangements. Parolees must submit home plans to parole officers before leaving the institution and arrangements must be worked out in advance. President Carter hired Amy's governess this way; why not try it?

If you don't find your answer in any of the above, perhaps it lies in your own family or neighborhood. If your daughter wants to use the family car on Saturday night, trade her X hours of housekeeping for driving privileges. If your son wants a new stereo set, suggest he earn it by chores. Trade chores with your husband. If that doesn't work and you have a friend whose husband likes to work around the house, ask her what she'll trade for his helping you. Or if you don't want to hassle your husband, children, and neighbors, find a friend who likes to do the work you hate and trade off jobs regularly. If you also swap checks, you will be building up social security benefits.

If you want to trade your services as housekeeper to get what you need, how do you start? Try some of the above suggestions in reverse. Check out local newspapers and magazines; advertise; post notices, talk to clergy, friends, counselors. Pass the word. Some of the best arrangements happen by word of mouth. Once you find your barter half, spell out your needs and explore his. When you have set the terms, spell everything out in a written contract, specifying hours, duties, expenses, reimbursements, use of property, and so on. If there is the slightest doubt in your mind, put everything on a trial basis and set a deadline. If it doesn't gel, shake hands, part company, and start searching again.

Housekeeping may be one of the easiest ways to get from where you are to where you want to be: out of marriage, into marriage, out of town, through college, getting jobs with celebrities, or gaining experience to write a best-seller.

But if you're middle-aged and have always wanted to run away with the circus, it may not be the best time to go. If you've lost your figure and are not the world's greatest acrobat, watch out. You may find yourself cleaning up after the elephants!

Housing

> "If you would love me, and have me for your companion and playfellow, and let me sit by your table and eat from your plate and drink from your cup and sleep in your little bed," the Frog Prince promised the little princess, "I will fetch your golden ball from the well."

Thus began one of the most familiar housing barters in fairy tales, which, as everyone has been led to believe, will, after much pathos, come to a happy ending. Thumbelina traded cooking, housekeeping, and storytelling with Fieldmouse for a warm place to stay for the winter; and everyone knows how the prince in *Sleeping Beauty* traded a kiss for a kingdom.

In real life such barters often go awry. Human nature has a tendency to renege on, or forget, promises; expectations are not always the same; conditions change. Therefore, to make sure barters are as sturdy as you wish your housing to be, be certain the terms of the agreement are in writing before you move in or sign on the dotted line.

Because shelter is a necessity of life, many people have a tendency to equate it with dollars. Nothing could be further from the truth. Housing is all around you, often available for the asking. What you get depends on where you look and what you are willing to trade for it, as well as where you want it to be. For instance, if you are elected president of the United States, you automatically acquire the White House for at least four years. Clergy? The parish house (as long as you observe the rules). A nun? The convent. Presidents of companies and universities receive residences as part of, in addition to, or in place of pay, as do interns, resident craftsmen, and resident scholars—not to mention inmates of prisons, institutions, and brothels. Expectations, as you can see, are an important part of the plan.

Happily, quality is winning out over mediocrity in our society, and many foundations and companies are discovering that if they provide the perfect environment as part of a job, they will attract more highly qualified employees. When Roy Slade recently resigned as director of the prestigious Corcoran Gallery of Art to become president of Cranbrook Academy of Art in Michigan, Washington was aghast. Why would anyone leave the center of culture to go to an academic post 16 miles from Detroit? Mr. Slade was only too glad to provide the answer. In addition to money, security, an academic schedule, and a chance to return to painting, he received as part of the terms of his contract a magnificent five-bedroom house designed by Eliel Saarinen, with formal courtyard and a 40-foot studio for his use. "I'll have time to paint," said Slade. "I feel like a preacher who hasn't had time to pray."

During the Depression, when money was hard to come by, actors performed at the Barter Theater in Virginia in return for food and shelter (see Entertainment). Thousands of murals were painted in public buildings by artists whose token pay was offset by community living accommodations. And in Boston, Massachusetts, instead of welfare, men received rent checks, hand-delivered, with a note telling them where to work that week.

In Russia almost all apartment rentals are handled through barter. Casual renting is rare. Applying for an apartment through regular channels can mean waiting for years. In Moscow, a city of more than 7 million population, the Main Bureau of Exchange makes about 70,000 such arrangements a year. Although it keeps file cards of listings at its office and publishes a weekly sixty-four-page *Exchange Bulletin,* individuals have found that one-to-one deals are not only faster but more reliable, so on weekends they walk the courtyard outside the bureau with a card affixed to their clothing which lists the advantages of what they have to offer. Such exchanges may involve as many as twenty-eight different links before completion, taking over a year to arrange. To offset this delay, and because such arrangements may be complex, those in the greatest hurry resort to illegal middlemen who charge a fee to speed up the process. When prospects decide that a deal looks hopeful, they inspect each other's premises before beginning the tedious paperwork needed to complete the transaction.

The best thing about bartering for housing in a democracy is that such rules and regulations don't exist. The sky is the limit. The only thing that can tie you down is a lack of your own imagination. So stop now, and ask yourself some questions to see where you are:

a. You already have housing but don't know what to do with it.
b. You have housing but it's not what you want.
c. You have housing but want more.
d. You want to improve on what you have by sharing the work and/or responsibility.
e. You don't want to own your own house; you want to live in somebody else's house on your terms.
f. You've found the perfect estate in the country but someone else owns it and you lack the funds to buy it.

Decide where you want to go. What kind of housing would you like to have? Do you need it full- or part-time? In the city or country? Seasonally or occasionally? Do you really want to own it or would you prefer living rent free while someone else pays the bills? How much work or service are you willing to invest (there is a direct correlation between time and labor in effecting the best deals).

If you find you don't know the answers to any or all of these questions, start looking around you. Read real estate advertisements to learn the current market values so that you will recognize a good buy when you see it. Get on the mailing lists of auctioneers to see what prices property is commanding. Sometimes housing is someplace else waiting to be moved, or disassembled like an erector set, waiting to be put together elsewhere. Check the local Board of Education (which sells buses that can be transformed into vacation homes or temporary shelter while building; and furniture and materials that can be bartered for other things). Some cities, such as Baltimore, sell homestead houses for as little as $1 in return for restoring them. The highway department also sells off houses to anyone willing to move them. If you own land to which a house can be moved without major problems, the total cost may be only a fraction of its value. Highway departments will also let you strip interiors of houses slated for demolition and plants from the yards for landscaping. After houses are knocked down, you can have all the brick you can carry away before it is plowed under. Old bricks are easily cleaned by rubbing them together and look better than new in fireplace walls, terraces, and walks around older houses. If you don't see yourself as a scavenger, check out brick manufacturers. You may be able to get free bricks delivered from their graveyard of discontinued sizes for transportation costs.

As soon as demolition companies win a contract to tear down a building, they are open to offers for some or all of the contents. But in working out such transactions, make sure you are dealing with the person in charge. Get the deal in writing so that you won't be arrested for stealing and trespassing. However, someone else might try to steal the materials you have claimed, so pick them up as soon as possible after the deal is completed.

After waiting six months for an elaborately carved door in a house slated to be torn down for a post office, one of us received a phone call saying to be at the site at 6:00 A.M. the next day. She was, and after waiting until 9:00 A.M. for the foreman to appear, got the door for $8. She was also offered (because she was first in line) a Victorian railing for $10 but refused it because her house was Georgian. This was a mistake due to inexperience. She has since learned not to turn down anything, because everything is worth something to somebody else. She could have sold the railing for $200 cash or credit toward something she needed; or bartered it for materials needed in the restoration.

If you have adequate storage to take advantage of such opportunities, organize the space, trading off what you don't need for what you do; or amass enough materials to build a completely new house from old parts. Or store parts for someone else in return for labor. If you lack space, barter talent, services, or transportation to get what you need. Parts can be traded for labor or other parts; or to restoration experts and architects for consultation. Antique hardware, for instance, is in great demand. If you can't find a likely buyer in your own neighborhood, advertise in antique newspapers or enter flea markets as a seller, trading and selling off what you don't need for something else.

If you own a truck, haul for other people, or trade the use of your truck and/or services for something you want. Skills such as writing, art, manual labor, or telephone answering can be traded in man-hours for materials and services. More often than not, trading off what you don't want will free space that can be traded for something else. Once you learn a skill, teaching it to someone else is a valuable barter. If you are researching your property at the local courthouse or library, offer to do your neighbor's as well in return for a chore he can do for you.

If you come across a piece of equipment that you think you can use, going at a good price, but you don't know how to use it, buy it and find someone who does. Mal and Calla Rose moved to the West Virginia mountains a few years ago and lived in a tent until they bought a horse to skid logs and build a log house. They traded plowing for lessons in how to use the 1,600-pound horse and again to have its special harness made, gaining not only proficiency but two new friends. If you own a chain saw, you can get free wood to build your house in return for cutting firewood for the owner of the woods, or splitting what you cut with him fifty-fifty. If you take that wood to the nearest planing mill, you can get it planed free by paying the mill a percentage of footage.

Learn how to to take down barns. If you apprentice yourself to a barn specialist as free help, you'll discover how to do it in a day. Many farmers, faced with the need to dismantle buildings that have fallen into disrepair, don't have the time and will gladly trade materials involved if you agree not to leave a single piece on the property. Many old barns are made of chestnut, rare in today's market and valuable barter. The wide boards used in barns make fabulous flooring; beams can be used as structural elements or cut in half to suggest beamed ceilings. Siding makes excellent kitchen cabinets, closet doors, or paneling for a room that needs plaster. Stones in foundations can be reused; plowshares turned into door handles; hardware reused or traded for something else. Or, if you are really industrious, after moving everything to your place, rebuild it as a barn or a house. Or trade what you don't need to a quality contractor in return for use of his equipment. Use surpluses constructively. One editor, recently returned from the Far East with a supply of oriental rugs, traded them for services needed in restoring his townhouse.

Suppose what you need belongs to someone else; determine what the owner will take in trade for it. If he is a car dealer, send him prospects. A doctor? Maybe he needs a housesitter while he is on vacation. A realtor? Give him ideas for new ways to sell listings. A contractor? Offer to stay with his model homes while he contacts prospects. In some instances it's best to come right out and state the deal; in others, it's better to warm up the prospect with favors (sometimes for as long as a year) before getting down to business.

If you already own your land, use it as down payment for mortgage money to build your house. Or buy a house half done, trading your labor to pay off half the price. (This can also save on annual taxes where appraisals are based on the purchase price.) Being your own contractor can save 15 to 50 percent of the total price, depending on how much you do yourself and what you subcontract. Get bids in writing and insist that subcontractors charge by the job rather than the hour; make sure they are insured against accidents so that a lawsuit doesn't wipe out your profits. Once you begin, don't deviate from the plans or expenses will mount. If you apply for and get a contractor's license, you may be able to get as much as 50 percent discount at appliance and hardware stores. Keep track of all sales tax you pay for materials so you can deduct it from federal taxes (additional savings in the cost).

If you don't own land, look for property with at least one house on it in order to get better mortgage terms from the bank. Fix up that house, then either sell it off with a portion of the land for a price equal to your investment, or rent it for depreciation and income. Either way, you get the rest of the land on which to build your house—free.

Or buy a larger house than you need and turn the space you don't use into apartments, giving you a profit, depreciation, and free rent and utilities. Many New York brownstone rooming houses have been renovated into cooperative apartments. Owners live in one and sell the others, recovering the initial investment after two are sold—the third is clear profit and future income (depending on how it is financed). Many properties have more than one house or building. A tenant house can be renovated for sale or rental; barns can be transformed into apartments. If you need additional help, trade off free rent in one of the units in return for labor. One of the best ways to buy income property cheaply is to find a new use for an old white elephant. Ten years ago we discovered a former nursing home consisting of three large buildings plus a three-car garage on 27 acres of land. Everyone else saw it as a hospital. We saw it as a historic house that would make a gracious residence and two additional buildings some distance from the main house that could be transformed into six apartments in ninety days. Scrounging up the minimum down payment by borrowing on our life insurance, we made the deadline and have been living rent free in a fifteen-room mansion ever since.

It is entirely possible to get income property to maintain itself. When you do, you can trade it off for other properties or use its income to support additional purchases. If you know your antiques, it is possible to buy a house furnished (the price is often not that much more, considering the value of its contents) and select the best pieces to keep or sell; auction the rest of the contents at a yard sale, then sell off the house by auction or private sale, doubling or tripling your investment in a relatively short time.

As you learn to barter for housing and materials, you will begin to see things that others miss, or other ways materials can be used. Wood salvaged from old houses is more seasoned than new wood and in some cases rare. If you prefer new materials, seek out the advertising display houses in your area. They are great sources for new plywood, fiber glass, plastic, and similar materials used for booths and signs in trade shows and fairs. Even the leftovers and scraps are made of first-class materials. Sawdust obtained from such firms makes good mulch and compost for plantings. Back-door bins outside stores often contain all kinds of goodies. Dumps and landfills are also excellent sources for materials. Contractors haul in truckloads of roofing gravel. If you catch them before they dump it, it's just as easy to get them to unload in your driveway for paving. City street crews often dump large logs rather than take time to cut them up. Heavy items such as old stoves remain in barns because no one wanted to haul them away. Fixed up, they make marvelous heaters or trade-offs for other materials. Barns often contain stacks of window frames which can be converted into greenhouses or walled-in sun porches. Exterior shutters can be used inside on windows, or put together as doors and dividers or even paneling.

If you can't find ready sources of supply, advertise. One dentist bartered for nine-tenths of his dreamhouse by advertising for help in the local paper under Wanted. Other dentists barter oral repairs for house and auto maintenance on a regular basis (see Professionals). One musician lived rent free at a summer theater colony while composing music, but when he went into business for himself, he lost his accommodations. After sinking his nest egg into land, he discovered he couldn't afford the down payment on the trailer he needed in which to live while building his house. So he offered to write radio advertising jingles for a mobile home dealer in full payment for the first major installment and was accepted.

Perhaps you don't want the responsibility of ownership and prefer using someone else's property for as long as you like. Tracy Perez of Vassalboro, Maine, found her answer by offering to paint a wall mural for a city friend in exchange for six weeks of urban living. The Positions and Situations column in *Mother Earth News* matched up a young New England couple with a California widow. The couple paid for six months' stay in California by cleaning and fixing up the widow's property, while she provided them with country living and down-home cooking. If you restore houses for others on a regular basis, you are usually allowed to live in them rent free during construction.

Or you could rent a large apartment and sublet to others of your choice, for a total rent that permits you to live rent free. Be a companion to an elderly person, or secretary to an author who can't type. Offer to do maintenance on a regular basis in an apartment house in return for a free apartment. The manager of an apartment house usually receives a free apartment and sometimes maid service. The usual yardstick is that if you manage over eighteen apartments, you will also be paid a salary; how much depends on the quality of the complex and the available profits of the owner. Another way to achieve free rent is by renting two unfurnished apartments. Furnish one with your old furniture, renting it for double or—if it's in a great neighborhood and your furniture is smashing—even triple, using the profits to furnish your own apartment. This is also a great way to earn your way through college. Instead of renting a room, lease a big house and take in students. With any degree of management, depending on what school you attend, you'll make enough to pay your tuition.

If you don't like to be in charge but have extra room at your disposal, form a commune. Well-established cooperative households are no longer considered hippie. They are excellent ways to share the rent and provide a generation mix while finding friendly help with the costs and chores.

Housesitting is another way to live rent free, depending on whether you do it once a year or on a regular basis. Some owners insist that the sitter pay half the costs, but most pay for everything, figuring it is good protection for their valuables. The biggest problem here is finding the first job. Approach someone leaving town and make an offer. Call college housing offices, check out newspaper advertisements under Houses to Let; place your own ad, put up posters or notices in conspicuous places; inquire among realtors. Be prepared with references, and on each job, get terms in writing to protect yourself. Determine whether you want a house or prefer apartment living (it pays to specialize). Decide how much yard work or maintenance you are willing to do. Find out if any restrictions exist (can you entertain?). If your occupation is one that can be done anywhere (writing, painting, or composing music), bartering is a great way to travel at someone else's expense. One young couple was hired by a wealthy family who owned several homes. Their job included travel expenses to the off-season house as well as use of a sailboat. College or university towns are ideal locations for housesitting jobs, as professors take lengthy sabbaticals. Travel light, and plan assignments ahead so that you can move directly from one to another (cities provide more opportunities for such activity). Try to move in while the owner is still there (preferably a week before his departure) so that you know how everything works and where everything is.

Or how about living in an experimental home? Many universities and ecological groups are developing alternate-energy housing. Find out where they are and volunteer to live free as a resident engineer and chart keeper. Or offer to live in a development model home in return for showing and maintaining it. Your presence will be insurance against vandalism.

If you know farming and long for the country, become a tenant farmer. You will receive free rent, usually a separate tenant house, free utilities, half a beef each year, often a car or truck, as well as $150 a week pay. If you are a skilled trainer of horses, you can barter your talent for free housing or even part ownership of a horse farm.

Want a downtown location for your business or office? Offer to decorate a store on a regular basis for office or shop space. Or, if you purchase a new type of prefab, ask the manufacturer for a discount on the purchase price in return for showing it to prospects on a regular basis. Get a free apartment in a historic building in return for being caretaker and tour guide. Some historical societies provide living quarters in return for managing a shop or cleaning house on a regular basis.

Organizations are notorious barterers (see the chapter of the same name). Some get free rent at fairgrounds by listing their activity as educational or paying the management with a percentage of profits. Others get historical surveys done by architectural students in return for providing them with living accommodations. When John D. Rockefeller was restoring Williamsburg, he discovered that the powder magazine in the center of town belonged to a branch of the Association for the Preservation of Virginia Antiquities. The only way he could get it was by buying the Rolfe-Warren House in Surry, Virginia, and trading for the powder magazine.

The National Trust for Historic Preservation exchanged the restoration and refurbishing of a gatehouse at Lyndhurst for free rent, as well as the restoration and refurbishing of the tenant house at

Woodlawn for a rent consideration. When state historical societies have only enough money to complete the exterior of a building, they often give life tenancy to individuals who agree to complete the interior. If you have a furniture collection that suits a historic house that doesn't have the correct furnishings, make an offer and you may be able to move in within the month; or if you live in a historic house complete with antiques, you can sign it over to a foundation in return for life tenancy.

With time and experience, you will learn which housing barters can be sealed with a handshake and which need to be spelled out in writing. There are times when the open-ended barter of friendship is worth more than acquiring the king's castle on the mountain. If there is the slightest doubt in your mind that a condition will not be met, or if you feel the intent of the parties differs (especially if more than one other party is involved), don't leave it to chance—get it in writing.

If God had written down the terms of Adam and Eve's occupancy in the Garden of Eden, they might never have eaten that apple, been evicted, and changed the course of history . . . but that's another story.

Information

I've Got a Secret

Informational barter ranges from the one-to-one exchange of "I'll tell you if you tell me," to plea bargaining, where a defendant furnishes information in return for his freedom, protection, or conviction on a lesser charge.

Scientists trade information for future business and professional contacts and for co-authorship in research papers; and on a regular basis scientific agencies that must know what others are doing exchange information. In legal cases attorneys tell each other what their clients want in order to speed up settlement and keep disputes out of court. Information for many of these chapters was obtained from specialists in return for writing a speech, lecturing a class, an introduction, a meal, or even the promise of a free copy of this book (which demonstrates that some of our experts have developed a finer sense of bartering than those who were introduced to it for the first time).

Experience (another form of information) is traded in business in return for formulas, patent rights, or contacts; and on farms for labor. Students on internships research for educational credits (see Education). Foundations trade their experts (who are actually walking information files) to the government in return for prestige, influence, or favors; they render research and market studies to preferred companies to gain an edge over competition (see Taxes).

There is also the implied barter, where information is "volunteered" and the "you owe me" is clear but never stated, as in the hot tip in a horse race, the warning of price increases in industry, or advance notice of changes in design that will make current models obsolete.

An acceleration in this area, when companies trade price information to keep prices up or down, is called price-fixing and is illegal; so is memorizing formulas to sell to competitors for money or a percentage of profits, or threatening to divulge information in order to influence a politician's vote.

Antique dealers searching for specific items reciprocate for information on buyers, sellers, and merchandise—sometimes for a percentage, a choice of something from their shop, or a future favor.

The IRS pays for information on tax evaders by rewarding an informer with a percentage of their gain. Testimony in court (another form of informational barter) is sometimes delivered for revenge, favors, or immunity.

Boy Scouts conduct tours at World's Fairs (imparting information on the sights) in return for badges and free admission. Preservation groups provide free information and consultation in return for protecting historical properties. Celebrities appear on talk shows free or at reduced rates in return for the chance to impart information on books, movies, or causes. Senior citizen organizations operate community referral services to be a part of the action.

Informational barter exists on every level of private and public life, with political defections about as far as you can go. Like the information itself, the price paid for it varies with the political winds. When Jimmy Carter moved into the White House and his cousin Hugh was assigned to trim the fat from the White House budget for office supplies, everything from limousines to newspaper subscriptions became newly scarce, therefore valuable, and barter became a White House staple. As the *Washington Post* reported, a freeze on yellow legal pads drove one staffer to barter information to government agencies, using legal pads as the medium of exchange.

As mousetrap methodology would have it, if you have the right information (or the right office supplies), the world will beat a path to your door. In some cases, though, that knock on the door could be your competitor, your boss, the FBI . . . or the IRS.

Land, Real Estate, and Mineral Rights

Landing Land Through Barter

"This was what I prayed for: a plot of land not too large, containing a garden, and near the house a fresh spring of water, and a bit of forest to complete it."

—HORACE

Man began bartering for land the day he arrived on earth and hasn't stopped since. Manhattan was obtained for beads. In the early history of our country, men traded gold, furs, and mineral rights for land and sometimes, although it was not officially recorded as such, marriage.

Man cannot live without land. Better than money in the bank, a needed resource for life and a basic factor of economic production, land has always been one of the fastest routes to power, prestige, and wealth. Men have lost lives discovering it and fighting wars over it; landed gentry married to keep it; land barons became notorious for grabbing it. Even the children's game "King of the Mountain" teaches and reinforces the concept of getting land and holding on to it as long as humanly possible.

Uncle Sam, the largest landowner in the United States since he outbartered the Indian, discovered early in his career that giving away land was one of the fastest ways to get jobs done. He gave land to Lafayette for volunteering in the Revolutionary War; to citizens for service above and beyond the call of duty; and to veterans of early wars for military service. Under the Homestead Act, the head of a family over twenty-one years of age was given 160 acres in return for living on it for five years, cultivating a portion, and making improvements. Land grant colleges (which today award over 40 percent of the Ph.D.'s conferred in the United States) received federal land for offering courses in agriculture and mechanical arts.

The best deals have always been those that don't involve money. Arthur Cohen, who operates on a larger scale than William Zeckendorf at his zenith, is a master of mortgaging out properties (borrowing the full amount and perhaps more of the development cost). Cohen, who has parlayed a $25,000 investment to over $200 million in a few years and whose Arlen Realty & Development Corporation's assets total approximately $1.2 billion, was quoted in *Fortune* as saying: "It never made any difference whether the thing had an equity requirement of a million dollars or twenty million dollars, because I didn't have either. Having no money at all, there was no limit on what I could do, because to do anything I had to create value and so generate all the capital I needed."

Good advice for anyone seeking land. In bartering for real estate it pays to think big and not let money get in the way of expectations. What do you want? Where is it? Who owns it? What are his needs? How can you meet them? Or if that answer is not readily available, what land do you know of with problems that you can use your brainpower to solve? Some of the largest land developers have become millionaires by packaging land deals, using their own brainpower as equity in combination with other people's money, often splitting profits, two-thirds to the investors and one-third to themselves as entrepreneurs.

To swing large deals, realtors frequently take back commission in stock, part ownership, or a second mortgage. Doing so gives them control, improves cash flow, increases tax advantages, and provides steady income in lean years. In developing such transactions they accept deals from the buyer or the seller, depending on who has the better credit rating (to ensure the success of the deal) or the greater need (increasing profits).

Owning land and real estate provides tax advantages, while trading it (versus selling) eliminates having to pay capital gains. When realtors or investors use up depreciation on a property, they trade it off for other real estate, on which they start taking depreciation all over again from the top. If they can't find an even trade, they may take two smaller pieces for a larger one, or one plus cash; or arrange a multiple trade with several other brokers through a nationwide network of brokerage pools and exchange brokers.

Such real estate barters are used as a safeguard against taxes on capital gains, as a financial hedge during high-income years, and to acquire adjoining tracts of land for development or industrial sites; to consolidate holdings in a single area; or to buy up blocks of low-income property for future restoration. Some developers are constantly on the lookout for older apartment buildings whose existing zoning permits them to build high-rise apartments on the same site at no additional land cost. More often than not, the easiest way to acquire them is through bartering a property whose surface value *appears* to be greater. Trading off and up helps increase income, improve holdings, and dispose of problem properties.

It's not always a case of "what you sees you gets." Many real estate barters involve rights under, on, and over land. If a company wants to trade $100,000 in coal rights for stock options owned by another company, it may label the property "forest land." The firm that gives up the stock options knows it has a new product coming on the market in two years that will drive up the price of its stock. However, in the meantime, it needs the money to develop its product. The coal does not show up on the books until it starts mining. In the meantime, the other company has the money to invest in its new product.

Some large companies buy land from owners, then lease it back to them for farming, renewing leases until the land is ready for development. Large developers can band together using this tactic to squeeze out farmers, holding onto the property until it is annexed by a nearby town, making it eligible for water and sewer at taxpayers' expense, and increasing its resale value many times over.

One lumber company traded 1,000 acres of land in West Virginia to a North Carolina company in exchange for a pine timber tract. The North Carolina company owners originally planned to build houses on the land, until they discovered it had excellent water. They are now negotiating with a beer company for a sale or trade, because the site is ideal for a distillery. A limestone quarry, fallen into disuse when processing furnaces in steel mills were electrified, was on its way to extinction until a young engineer discovered the stone was ideal for concrete and beds of subways. His ingenuity in land use paid off twofold: first promoted by the subway company, he now sits on the board of directors of the quarry.

Timing, versatility, experience, knowing where experts are when needed so that you can obtain reliable opinions fast, adding up and analyzing information, utilizing assets, keeping the momentum going, eliminating drawbacks or problems as they arise or before others realize they exist are also important tools in land and mineral right barters. Being able to add two and two and come up with six instead of the usual four pays off when opportunity knocks. If Joe Hirshhorn had believed Mark Twain's adage that "a gold mine is a big hole with a liar at the other end," he might not have struck it rich and gone on to amass the fabulous art collection that he has since given to the American people. When a geologist from Preston East Dome (PED) in northern Ontario divulged his theory on gold deposits to Joe, he bet $25,000 of his money on a drilling program. At the time PED was out of funds and its stock certificates were selling for less than 5¢ on the Toronto Exchange. Using its theory and Joe's money, PED struck gold 25 feet from the old shaft and by the mid-1950s was grossing an annual $2.5 million. The relationship flourished, and in 1952 when François

Jaubin told Joe his theory of uranium deposits, Joe put up $30,000, cutting in Jaubin for 10 percent. Fifty out of fifty-six core samples showed uranium, and Joe offered PED a fifty-fifty deal. PED agreed to put up the men, Geiger counters, tents, sleeping bags, food, and lawyers as its share of the ante and staked out 14,000 claims in six weeks over 56,000 acres of land—one of the most fabulous finds in Canadian history.

Sometimes the wealth is right on the surface, but no one recognizes it. The owner of a mountain hotel couldn't get bus tours to go out of their way to stop at his place. He learned that 180 acres near the new highway were coming up for sale. He didn't have the money, but he did have an idea. Taking an option on the land, he got a contract from the highway department for the topsoil on the property (enough to pay the total price), used that as down payment on the land, the loan from the bank to pay off the capital gains, and the remainder to build a large restaurant for bus tours (whose foundation had been graded perfectly, courtesy of the highway department). Once the buses stopped on a regular basis he fed them good food at reasonable prices, along with literature on his hotel and charms of the region, offering a free ride up the mountain to see the view and enjoy dessert. Before long, many of the passengers were coming back, making their stays longer and more frequent. Another realtor traded off a downtown location for an old wharf, converted fishing shacks and boat buildings to air-conditioned apartments, sold them individually as condominiums, and doubled his money by the time one-third of the units were sold.

When a Texas contractor inherited the family farm which happened to be in the middle of a good residential district, instead of building more houses, he got it zoned for a shopping center, and after obtaining contracts from businesses for space in the complex, used them as collateral for a construction loan from the bank. To fill the shopping center fast, he offered low rent for the first five years, plus a percentage of profits above that amount to be paid to him. Prospective tenants liked his "you-can't-lose" deal. As soon as the complex was filled, he built expensive housing on the outer fringes of the acreage, filling up the space nearby with quality townhouses and apartments to build up profits for his lessees. Bartering inheritance and know-how, combining it with hard work and follow-through, using other people's money and business acumen, he now owns his own town. Other builders sell shopping centers but retain ownership of the land to cash in on future appreciation; or offer to build a large department store at a reduced cost for the right to build, own, and rent satellite stores around it.

Trading services is another way of acquiring land and businesses. While on Broadway, actor William Wayne McMillan Rogers III, known as Trapper John on *MASH,* did the bookkeeping in a New York saloon and ended up owning one-third of the establishment. A Washington, D.C., accountant traded his management skills to an Annapolis architectural firm in return for design work and is now a full partner. If you are skilled with horses, trade your know-how to the owner of a horse farm in return for free housing, acreage, or part of the business. A skilled contractor can barter his skills with a landowner in return for half ownership of the developing firm, then subcontract all the work without owning a single piece of equipment. Other contractors work out deals with local suppliers, charging the customer less for the job or by the hour and getting a 10 percent rebate from suppliers on all materials ordered for the job. Often when a developer or builder finds himself low on cash, he will barter land for paving, architectural plans, decorating, advertising, materials, clearing land, or plumbing and electrical services.

If a large tract of land bought for development contains extra buildings which have to be torn down, an enterprising individual can acquire the land he wants in return for dismantling the buildings, selling off pieces and parts, or rebuilding them elsewhere as a single building. Or he can contract to restore the major house on the property as a clubhouse in return for land and other buildings.

A farmer who doesn't use all his land is often open to offers that will enable him to maintain it. He may give you a lot of land on which to build a house if you guarantee him X number of years' labor in payment. He may let you farm the entire acreage in return for one-third of the crop. Or he may deed part of it to you in return for rebuilding or repairing its buildings; if he has many properties requiring maintenance, he could trade you one in return for managing the rest over an extended period of time. (For more bright ideas, see Farming.)

A retired person who wants to stay in his family home but can no longer physically do the work involved is often eager to arrive at some solution. If you know of such a person, find out what his needs are (i.e., transportation, managing a business) and he may have the answer to yours (a lot of land next door, or part ownership in a land deal).

If you hear of a large piece of land or business that has been on the market for a long time, find a new use for it, sell the owner on the idea, get backers and arrange financing in return for a piece of land or part ownership of the business. Or, if you have good credit, buy the whole thing yourself, arrange the same deal, and take all the profits—in land or part ownership. Another way to obtain land free is to buy more acreage than you need (the price per acre goes down as the number of acres goes up). If it has an existing house, you will get better terms on the mortgage. Renovate the house and sell it with a portion of the acreage for at least the price you paid for the entirety, then build the house you want on the land that is left. Oftentimes, older places have tenant houses, stores, gate-houses, and stables that can be converted into income property or sold off separately for more than the original price. You say you don't have any money and the lot you want is in a subdivision? Work it off on weekends. If you're so crazy about the development, you may make a great salesman. Ask the owner if you can have your lot free in return for selling ten others (again, get the agreement in writing first).

Many developers are coming up with their own barters. Lake Arrowhead, Georgia, has developed an annuity plan which guarantees purchasers their money back after ten years. If they pay cash, the $10,000 lots costs only $7,150. If they take terms, they pay 15 percent down and the remainder over ten years at 8¾ percent interest. One year after the lot is paid for, they receive a paid-up annuity which gives them $1,000 a year for the next ten years, so that after twenty-one years they own the lot and have all their money back (except interest, which is tax deductible). Under the blanket policy purchased by the developers, owners can pass the annuity on to their heirs or give it to a charitable organization, taking an immediate tax deduction.

Or perhaps you are looking for a place to park your trailer for the weekend? Dream big, find the exact spot that fills your soul, check out land records to locate the owner, then offer to share the trailer with him as a guesthouse or traveling vacation home (he may be looking for a way to get away!) in return for free rent at the site. But work out details in writing to ensure a healthy long-lasting relationship. Perhaps you don't own a trailer but enjoy long walks at the seashore. If you live nearby, offer to help with maintenance or be the local rental agent in return for using a trailer occasionally. Your presence on a regular basis is good protection against vandalism. If you prefer the mountains, find the perfect place and owner, then offer to help with road repair, wood clearing, or maintenance in return for two weeks free a year (of your choice, naturally).

If you already own land and it's in the wrong place, or a house you want to trade for land, or a business you'd like to quit or swap for a retirement home, advertise in the local paper where you want to go. If that doesn't work, advertise at home. Or ask your local realtor to provide you with the names of reliable real estate exchange brokers at your chosen destination.

The Original Yankee Swoppers Column in *Yankee* Magazine (Dublin, N.H. 03444) prints land "swops" free of charge. Send in your ad of no more than thirty-two words at least three months in advance. Each month they draw and print 100 acceptable swops at random. Or subscribe to the magazine; you may find exactly what you want waiting in someone else's backyard. Also check *Mother Earth News* (P.O. Box 70, Hendersonville, N.C. 28739).

Although some land barters are illegal (trading information on future road construction to speculators in return for favors, or buying land while a member of a planning board to resell at a profit after rezoning), land is still one of the best investments around, whether it is acquired for money or for barter. Small wonder it's referred to as *real* estate.

Man can't reproduce it. Neither can he expand what is already here. He may reclaim it from under water or rearrange what's already on earth, but as the realtors like to say, "God isn't going to make any more land." If you want a piece of the action, your own land of milk and honey, there is no time like the present to begin. What better way than to take a leaf from Adam and stake out a claim—through barter?

See also: Big Business, Farming, Food, Housing.

Law

Legal Tenders

Barter is used in law much as cards are played in poker: to get as many chips as possible on your side of the board; gain the upper hand; set up the other side; bluff the opposition; put them at a disadvantage; force them into making concessions; save up points to play off in a crunch or swing the game in your favor at the right psychological moment; or use as insurance to keep your adversary from trying surprise future plays.

For instance, in negotiations between a couple seeking a divorce, the wife is usually advised by her lawyer not to give the husband permission to leave or consent to a voluntary separation, so that he will have to pay points from his side to gain her consent. Even if she does not want or need alimony and may indeed be planning on remarrying as soon as the divorce is final, the threat of alimony is a powerful card to use as barter for something she wants—like the house. Once she is awarded alimony, unless she remarries, the only way a husband can get out of it at a later date is by returning to court (additional expense) or trading off some of his assets (part ownership of the house). Says one divorce lawyer, "It is worth everything to the husband to get the wife to waive alimony."

If a husband has planned ahead (sometimes by as much as twenty years) and not put anything he owns in his wife's name, and she needs bartering leverage, she in turn is advised to remove assets belonging to her husband to an undisclosed, insured location *in her name only* to use as future barter power. This is one reason why wives sometimes stage commando raids on safe vaults to take securities and ownership papers; or remove all the furniture from the house, or inventory from the business. To get what he believes is rightfully his, the husband must go to court and prove it, or settle out of court (taking less time) by agreeing to a cash settlement for marital rights or to pay alimony for life (or until the wife remarries).

Because alimony is such a strong trading card, husbands are sometimes advised by lawyers to ask for custody of the children (guaranteed to strike fear in a mother's breast), even if it is the last thing on earth they are seeking. Mothers usually do not want to part with their children and often need child support as income until they can learn marketable skills or remarry. The husband who institutes such a custody suit can dismiss it as soon as the wife waives alimony. Conversely, if a wife does not want or need alimony, she is advised to ask for token alimony ($1 a year or a month) as insurance against future needs or when she needs a bartering point. (If she becomes incapacitated at some future date, the husband will then have to support her.)

In such transactions timing is vital. A winning card must be played before it is taken away or loses its power, but never before it has built up enough pressure. To accumulate additional trading cards, lawyers counsel wives to hide income (so that they can request more alimony) and to ask for the children even if they don't want them, trading these points later on for something else. In such barters it is important not to let the other side know what you want or how badly you need it. Otherwise, either party can return at a later date (especially if there has been no written or court property settlement) and claim half ownership in anything the other party had before the divorce. For instance, the husband can claim half the wife's furniture to force the sale of the jointly owned house; or the wife can use her alimony as partial payment to buy him out of joint assets.

In criminal cases, where the defendant is known to be guilty, the state's attorney will often suggest that he plead guilty in return for a lighter sentence because going to trial will usually bring harsher penalties.

Legal plea bargaining—or the practice of getting a defendant to plead guilty by reducing the charge to save the time and expense involved in a trial—is handled several ways: to reduce the charge, press for a lesser charge, drop the charge completely, or agree to a lighter sentence.

If the state does not have enough evidence to prove guilt, plea bargaining assures a guilty verdict otherwise not guaranteed. Judges are also more lenient with a defendant who volunteers information.

In governmental investigations many underworld figures bargain for freedom by informing on their co-conspirators. Unfortunately, these barters often turn sour when the informant is killed off by his mob to prevent his testifying in court.

If a defendant pleads guilty without a trial, charges may be reduced or dropped in return for turning "state's witness." In the famous Watergate case John Dean originally wanted immunity from all prosecution in return for testifying, but he eventually consented to inform in return for being judged guilty on only one count: conspiracy to obstruct justice.

Spiro Agnew resigned from the vice-presidency, pleading no contest to a single count of tax evasion in return for the government's dropping all other federal charges and recommending against a jail term. In one of the most astute plea bargainings on record, Agnew was fined only $10,000 and put on unsupervised probation for three years. The facts of the case were never made public and he was allowed to continue to protest his innocence; a neat barter.

After a recent theft of $547,000, the two gunmen and two receivers were not identified by the bank teller. With no witnesses, the state's evidence was too circumstantial to stand up in court. The four were offered a deal. In return for giving back $400,000 in twelve hours, the ringleader and the receivers were set free, the other robber received a minimal five-year sentence, and the group was free to divide the remaining $147,000.

Clifford Irving and his wife Edith were charged with grand larceny, conspiracy, mail fraud, and possession of forged documents connected with the biography of Howard R. Hughes which could have amounted to a hundred years apiece. Instead, Irving received two and a half years and a $10,000 fine and Edith two months of a two-year sentence.

In 1974 Harry L. Sears, Republican leader of the New Jersey Senate and chairman of the Nixon campaign in New Jersey, testified against former Attorney General John Mitchell and former Secretary of Commerce Maurice Stans. He was granted total immunity from charges of conspiracy, obstruction of justice, and perjury in connection with alleged attempts to obstruct a federal investigation of financier Robert L. Vesco.

Herbert Kalmbach, Richard Nixon's personal attorney, pleaded guilty to minor charges: a felony charge of soliciting $2.8 million for an illegally formed 1970 campaign committee, and a misdemeanor charge of offering an ambassadorship in Europe in return for campaign contributions of $100,000. All other charges against him were dropped in return for his cooperation and disclosure of relevant information and documents.

On the lighter side of the law, it is possible to pay one's legal bills with talents that can include anything from secretarial skills to free medical advice.

Members of barter groups like MCB Systems (Los Angeles, California) can pay for legal services by bartering their own services or merchandise for a slight charge to cover bookkeeping.

In personal injury cases, when the injured person is not in fact at fault but the evidence is not overwhelming to that effect, the insurance company may offer to settle out of court rather than take on the expense of going to court and losing the case, which would mean paying a larger settlement. By agreeing to settle out of court, they are not admitting guilt; and the injured party, by taking settlement, sidesteps the chance of losing it all. One insurance company with a recalcitrant client settled with the plaintiff in exchange for his not telling the company's client that he had won.

Discrimination cases are extremely difficult to prove in court, which is why many are settled out of court. The person discriminated against knows he is right, but in court it is hard to show how. The alleged discriminator knows this, but also realizes going into court can cost as much as $6,000 for three days (and attorneys lose money by going into court). Therefore, most companies prefer to settle out of court. Their first offer is usually the lowest. The person discriminated against figures out the odds (if the case is decided in his favor, he will win $30,000; if against him, nothing; therefore, if the company offers him $7,000 as they go in the courthouse door, it may be worth settling). Time is on the side of the person initiating the suit. The defendant must put up the ante in order to settle. Consequently, many legal barters in discrimination are not based on liability but are designed to forestall going to court and leaving the decision to the jury.

In credit cases where a client owes a creditor money, the creditor harasses him for a larger payment, then agrees to extend terms or take a lesser amount to avoid the debtor's declaring bankruptcy. Or, in marital cases where the husband beats up his wife and she wants a divorce but he doesn't, she is urged to press criminal charges against the husband, dropping them after he agrees to go along with divorce proceedings.

Drug violators who promise to join a rehabilitation program receive a lesser charge or charges against them are dropped completely; drivers admit guilt to speeding charges (it's hard to argue with radar) so that they can get a 641 (probation before verdict). Result: no fines, no points.

A judge agreed to waive a one-year prison sentence for a tax evader in Castro Valley, California, if he would agree to lecture to community groups on the perils of income tax evasion. It was a good barter until the speaker got carried away with his own jokes ("I sent the IRS 25¢ because I heard I could pay my taxes by the quarter!"). The judge warned him if he didn't clean up his act, he would go to jail. When comedy continued to take precedence over taxes, the judge stopped the laughter by reversing the barter and sending the evader to jail, where the former speaker is using his time to study tax law. Only time will tell which barter was better.

When Chief Justice Warren E. Burger learned he had to pay $25 for a seat in the Inaugural Parade (according to a *Washington Post* report on January 11, 1977), he said, "Then I'll charge Carter $50 to swear him in." A page in history that could have been improved by—a barter by Carter.

Livestock and Pets

Petting It Up

Do you remember when Boy, son of Jane and Tarzan, traded two baby lion cubs to a huntress for a flashlight? And how Tarzan tracked her down and gave the flashlight back because he knew she was going to put the cubs in a zoo and he thought it was wrong to commit them to such a fate?

There's a moral in that. Where animals are coming from as well as where they are going, and to whom, is important. Bartering animals, whether to enjoy as pets, to breed for money, or to raise for feed, presents pitfalls to be avoided or assessed carefully in advance. We've all known parents who sent home guppies as favors from a child's birthday party, or neighbors who "gave" kittens as "presents." Dealing with animals means dealing with life and requires the right timing, conditions, and permission.

What conditions will you trade to become an owner? Are you willing to nurse an animal back to health? There is an inverse ratio of condition to value that can work in your favor if you are willing to invest time and caring to provide the right living conditions. What kind of animal do you want? Do you want it for your very own, or are you willing to share ownership? Would you settle for maintaining someone's animal in return for privileges? What kind of experience can you offer? If you're a vet, you will have to trade less on this score than an inexperienced laborer. What do you have in land or materials that would make an attractive trade? What are the needs of the animal? What needs of its owner can you satisfy with barter?

Zoos trade animals all the time. Aquariums trade fish. A famous movie star once did a commercial for a pet food company in return for food for her fourteen dogs. (We don't know the ground rules for acquiring trained fleas but guess you would probably have to acquire and train a dog as the first step.)

What kind of housing is available at your place? If you have a barn, you could barter for a horse any time of the year, getting better terms during winter months when owners run out of feed. Being able to provide year-round housing could win you full or half ownership free. If you have fenced-in pasture, keep cattle for someone else in return for a percentage of their number. Hal Walker of Middletown, Maryland, is allowing an owner to graze two horses in his pasture for two years in return for two foals out of the first four born. When a New York teen-ager heard a neighbor could no longer care for his horse, she offered to take him. Since she was the only one with a large enough fenced-in yard and stable, she got him free. Getting up early each morning to train and exercise him, working afternoons at a horse farm for know-how, she trained him to become one of the best jumpers in New York State and in the next few years won prizes in every major East Coast show. When it came time to go to college, she had a built-in tuition plan, trading him to a Maryland breeder for enough money to pay for four years' education. By using her facilities to get a horse and bettering her barter with training, she got a college education.

If the animal you covet is on a farm, there are lots of chores a farmer needs help with and would accept as barter, such as weeding, harvesting, repairing, and tending on a regular basis. Explore his needs and see how you can meet them.

If you'd like a horse but don't have the accommodations, use those belonging to someone else. Stables and horse farms will trade board and lessons for help mending fences, cleaning stables, exercising, walking, or showing. You may start out trading for lessons or horse board and eventually become part owner. Many racehorses are owned by more than one person. Once a horse becomes a winner, breeding fees will more than pay his way. Breeding can also be traded for other favors and/or horses to improve the strain. In-town professionals who don't have the time or space for horses trade their services to a farmer for pasture and hay; to the blacksmith for shoeing; and to tack stores for equipment and supplies. The Farm Items and Livestock columns in newspapers regularly carry barter offerings (2 cattle for 500 bales of hay, for example). If you know horses and find one that needs care, offer to groom and care for it in return for ownership, paying a live foal as the full purchase price.

If you are an experienced trainer or jockey, you can trade your services for part ownership in a horse or even a horse farm. If you already own the horse and want to barter for food to feed it, trade off services (building or repairing a barn) for feed. Or try gleaning—ask farmers who live near you if you can pick up gleanings by hand in return for a half share (see Farming).

Working for a vet or a breeder will give you experience to trade and put you first in line for ownership on breeder's terms or first choice of animals that owners can no longer care for. You can own a registered dog free in return for letting the previous owner have the pick of a percentage of the litters. Carol Duffy of Stanfordville, New York, got her first Afghan hound this way and raised him to a champion, increasing the value of his stud fees, and so achieving more selectivity in his mates and better deals. Many owners of female dogs will offer pick of the litter to the owner of a male dog instead of stud fees. Or, if you know a dog in the neighborhood you especially like, talk to the owner. You may get pick of the next litter in return for dogsitting or walking his pet on a regular basis.

If the animal you want is in a pet shop, see if you can arrange payment by cleaning cages, raising food (mice), or waiting counter to pay off the credit.

Want fish in your pond? Call the local wildlife commission. It will stock your pond with free fish if you allow a limited amount of public fishing.

Or sheep? Locate a large sheep farmer at lambing season. If he has a large operation, he often can't spare the labor involved in raising cosset lambs (abandoned by their mothers). Offer to take as many as you think you can handle, returning half at weaning age. All it takes is a little bottle feeding—and you don't even have to change diapers!

Have you always wanted to raise bees for honey to replace the sugar in your diet? A live hive costs about $125. You can barter goods or labor to get one, but if you find a busy farmer whose crops need cross-pollination, he might trade you a share of his honey or hives in return for caring for them for him. Once you have the colonies and hives, you can rent them to producers of blueberries, cranberries, apples, and cucumbers, which also need cross-pollination at different times of the year. Take fruit instead of money, trade it on shares to someone to make preserves, or take the honey and fruit to the nearest farmers' market to trade for other food.

Rabbits can multiply into many barters and are easy to get if the owner is tired of caring for them (anytime but Easter). Once you get them moving in the right direction, they can be traded for chickens or to French restaurants for food credits, or sold to labs for research. Growers of pork will often trade a pig (live or ready for the freezer) in return for help at butchering time.

Food for animals can be procured by sharing your acreage with a farmer or helping with the chores. If the expense makes you feel as if you're feeding the local feed store, try shopping the back door of the grocery store after closing hours. Make a deal to pick up all produce thrown out each day, saving them the trouble and expense of taking waste to the dump. (But don't miss a day or you'll lose the deal.) Chickens, ducks, turkeys, and rabbits will love it, and your animal-raising neighbors will appreciate the excess, which can be bartered for some of your other needs.

Getting rid of animals is sometimes more difficult than acquiring them. Timing is also important. It's easier to trade off rabbits and chickens at Eastertime; reindeer at Christmas; or an elephant in the spring when he's outside eating grass. Try trading animals to the pet shop for other needs.

You say you want to start your own zoo? All it takes is one animal. Raise something no one else has and let the world beat a path to your door. Get "whatever it is" on breeder's terms, arrange the perfect environment, and let nature take its course, then trade off with every zoo in the country. As a basis of comparison for barters, here are a few of the going prices: Addax Antelope, $4,000; Przewalski Horse (in striped pajamas), $5,000; mute swan, $300; and mountain gorilla, $40,000. If that's too rich for your blood, how about a porcupine at $25?

Every so often someone gets a pet everyone else wants. Jim Wells had had his eye on an RCA trademark dog named Nipper on the top of a five-story warehouse for the past twenty-two years. Six years ago he started a campaign to get it. After winning the confidence of the management, convincing them that he appreciated the dog as much as they did, and that he would protect and cherish it, he got it for $1. Hiring a crane and truck, he hoisted the 1,707-pound white dog with cocked head and floppy black ears over to his place in Virginia, and no sooner had he gotten it there than the City of Baltimore wanted it back. What would Wells take?

"I've heard a rumor for years," he said, "of an old circus steam calliope gathering dust in an empty building in northeast Baltimore. That's the only thing I'll take in trade."

Baltimore has started the search.

Media

Spots Before Your Ayes

When Schick, Inc., found itself with 400,000 unsold units of a new product called Warm 'n Creamy, a hot-facial application marketing at $25, they were faced with several alternatives: discontinue the item with a resulting loss; cut the price (more loss); or sell at a negotiated price to a media barter firm in return for advertising time on radio and TV. Bartered in lots of 1,000 units at $25,000 air time, it was traded as giveaways and contest prizes.

A major car manufacturer, faced with unsold cars, unloaded over $50 million worth of inventory by the same route, processing the transaction through its advertising agency to guarantee a good time slot. The agency hired the barter company, which traded the cars for twice their value in TV and radio time spread over three to five years. The line of credit negotiated with the station went to the advertising agency to use as part of its regular media buying for the manufacturer, with the agency and the barter company splitting the commission. Cars were shipped through local dealers, who collected a fee from headquarters for preparing and picking them up. Without spending money, the inventory moved, everyone stayed in business, and the factory kept producing.

Large-scale media barter in the United States started in the mid-1950s to help TV improve its cash flow. Barter firms would buy a TV camera for a station or network in exchange for air time, which the firms then sold to businesses for cash. Many agencies during that time also "bought" prime time at a good barter rate for many years, putting them in the driver's seat on future deals. During the same period manufacturers were being strangled by large inventories. Short on cash, loaded with inventory, more and more major companies turned to barter to reduce storage costs, obtain advertising without cash, and keep their inventories moving. The resulting trade-offs, trade-outs, and due bills of what has become known as the reciprocal trade industry spawned additional barter agencies— many of them offshoots of the advertising companies that once looked down on the practice.

Anything that a media man's budget did not include could be bartered for: space, time, advertising, contest prizes, airline flights anywhere in the world, vacations at plush resorts, personnel, sports equipment, writing, artwork, even college educations.

When a former advertising man became sales manager for a small radio station, he discovered the station had a trade-out with a New York City hotel permitting him to schedule one week each month in New York and stay at the hotel while he called on advertisers. It saved the station the expense of having a New York sales rep; the hotel received free advertising on the local station; and when area people went to New York, the hotel was the only familiar name in the city.

By contacting any one of the hundreds of reciprocal trade media brokers in the United States, radio or TV stations can state their need and how much they are willing to trade for it, and pay a 15 percent commission to the broker to negotiate for them. Or they can bypass the commission and deal direct on a dollar-for-dollar basis. Each barterer must decide if he can do better on his own or through a broker.

When a station deals direct, it can be through a gentlemen's agreement. When a broker is the go-between, a contract is signed listing conditions, fees, and deadlines. Many stations have one-to-one trade-offs on a continuing basis from year to year. When radio owners deal direct, they can usually select where they want to go and push for extras such as food, drinks—everything except taxes, tips, cleaning, gratuities, and domestic air flights. Sometimes an owner may have to make five or six calls before he strikes a good deal, calling several chains and listings in the AAAA Directory before finding an arrangement. "When they say, 'No, we don't trade,' " one owner said, "it usually means, 'We haven't found what we want yet.' "

Calling a media broker is much like calling a travel agent—only you are faced with a bill of only 15 percent of the total (and this 15 percent is washed out as advertising expense). Most media brokers are one- or two-man shops, and the deal can start with a telephone call that goes: "I need a trip to Europe. What do you have?" But some phone calls end up going in the wrong direction. One media broker, when asked if he could get a "little auto" (meaning a $350 replica), arranged for an $8,000 coupé.

Broker barters must be used up in a year, and the time often goes by faster than expected. If a station manager isn't careful, he can lose $1,000 in air time by not keeping tabs on accumulated barters. Another way money is lost is by overestimating what winners of a contest will spend. In a recent promotional trip to New Orleans bartered at $1,500 for a prize in an auto show, a couple spent only $350 but the $1,500 had to be repaid in air time. Cruises are easier to estimate because the cost is predetermined and stations can specify in advance how much will be spent.

Trade-outs are usually used as prizes in promotions, but they can also be used as bait for advertising. For instance, if a local car dealer doubles his advertising, he is awarded a trip to Bermuda. Or the car dealer can offer the prize during an open house to lure new customers into his showroom. Top advertisers are given trips as Christmas presents which they can pass along to their customers or share with their families, getting free accommodations but paying their own airfare. Some of these hotel trade-offs include room only, while others will foot half the cost of food, or room and breakfast. Others again will absorb the entire bill, depending on how much they need advertising in the radio station's area.

Sometimes advertising exchanged for hotel accommodations doesn't advertise the hotel at all but is copy for a subsidiary of the chain, or even advertising for razor blades. Most stations retain the option to reject advertising if it does not fit in with their format (religious advertising, foundation garments, or rock festivals). Top advertisers usually insist that their advertising be in prime time. If the time the trade-out wants is already booked up, the owner must put it in an equal spot.

Bartered advertising must be treated the same as that for which money is paid. If national advertising is received as barter, the station owner usually lets local advertising agencies know he is handling it so that they can buy a "tag" to put on the end of the commercial. If it's a trip to a certain resort offered as a prize, a smart owner will send for posters and/or displays. More often than not, the resort will take out additional advertising in the local newspaper, promoting the contest as well as highlighting the region. Top-notch resorts may send a consultant or salesman with the display. If the trip is used in a shopping mall promotion, the mall will tagline store ads, or issue a special supplement in the local newspaper.

Because domestic airlines cannot trade out (ICC ruling), when a complete package is offered, foreign airlines are usually used.

Another form of barter is group tours used for sales incentives. The station contracts through a barter media man for twenty seats to Las Vegas. If a client buys a $1,000 radio time contract, he gets one seat; if he buys a $1,500 contract, he gets two seats.

These free ads are usually logged like regular advertising, then balanced as expenses to wash out taxes incurred. Barters are reported as revenues to the FCC and included as sales in the appropriate lines.

Another sort of barter takes place in programming big TV shows. Stations get shows free if they carry half the network ads. If a show has six ads, three are sold locally with three network ads carried. Or the show could sell two and give the station six. Baseball and football games are aired this way. The sending station broadcasts with six spots: two for a national advertiser and four sold locally, costing the station nothing for the game. Sometimes the sponsoring station pays for the line, sometimes the local station. When a station runs football from a larger station under such an arrangement, it picks up times for ads from cue sheets provided from the other station.

Any show produced by an individual or a station and videotaped can be offered to other stations on a barter basis. If the program is related in some way to a product, it can be the basis of a partnership between the packager and the product owner on a percentage of sales or a separate corporation partially owned by each. Some radio stations arrange their own packages: going to a theater and getting free tickets in return for advertising; arranging with a local bus company to provide transportation for free advertising and then giving away the tickets as station prizes, special promotions, or to favorite customers. A bus company may use its share of the advertising to form its own package, announcing a bus trip to Nashville and offering introductions to popular country music stars, whose music the radio station plugs as a tie-in with the production. Car dealers (see Autos) trade car leases and maintenance for air time, which they use to form their own packages tying in theaters and restaurants.

One of the neatest deals in recent TV barter was pulled off by Playtex. Rebuffed by TV stations who didn't want to carry undergarment ads, Playtex bought up a huge library of old movies, which they offered free to stations in return for free ads. If stations wanted the movies, it was the only way they could get them. A sound company provided the commercial sound effects and music for an exterminating firm in return for a number of spots. Other companies offer premiums; depending on the taste level of the station audience, this could range from autographed records to bonds.

Media brokers send out newspapers, mailing lists, and brochures, which many radio station owners keep as bonus selection material for local clients. One media company started a business similar to a credit card bank, charging members $100 to join, then accepting credits of air time, hotel accommodations, and vacations from members, which they advertised in their magazine. Another gambit is the air auction, but this runs into too much time because bids are logged as advertising. Since a station can do only eighteen commercial minutes in each hour, this is usually taken care of by saying, "This prize was donated by . . ."

Hotels often get into barter not because they need guests, but because they need decorating, air conditioning, office equipment, or even exterminating. There are sometimes limitations in hotel barter—reservations must be made for certain times of the week or year, or only on weekends. In some cases they can't be made until two weeks ahead of time, and if canceled must be paid just the same, with a minimum of $250 on each barter.

The best media barters occur when each party thinks he is getting the better deal. The only bad barter occurs when one is trying to take advantage of the other. "If I find out a company is doing money business with another area station, while hitting me for trade-outs," said one owner, "it's all over, and I expect money, too."

A bad barter that is taking place in radio-TV circles is the questionable "purchase" by barter of ARB survey diaries. Sent at random to viewers and listeners throughout the United States, they greatly affect the price stations can charge for advertising. One rating point nationwide represents 710,000 homes and is worth $1 million in advertising revenues. Sometimes an individual receives one in the mail and doesn't feel like taking the time necessary to fill it out, so he calls the nearest radio or TV station to ask what can be done with it. One major market radio station owner who admitted he bought one or two diaries regularly said, "Two diaries in my market can result in $150,000 in advertising revenues or more." In a county of approximately 100,000 population, there might be thirty-five diaries. If a station can procure only five, it can swing the percentages in its favor. If the ratings show it has the largest audience, it can charge more for advertising. Money doesn't change hands but barter does, in the form of a trip to Hawaii or a color TV set. A number of broadcasters have voiced strong protest against the Arbitron radio audience ratings survey because of these alleged irregularities, saying that in the case of buying diaries, dishonesty pays off in advertising revenues.

Another questionable barter is the fine line between payola, plugola, and barter. The consensus of opinion seems to be that legal deals are done on top of the table while illegal go under. If a disk jockey accepts something in return for playing a record a certain number of times each day without going through the station, it's payola. If he gives free advertising to an enterprise he owns, it's a conflict of interest. Because some stations encourage radio announcers to sell advertising time on their programs in return for extra benefits with the station, while other disk jockeys make side deals with promoters to plug their personal appearances at weekend affairs, illegal barters are difficult to prove when irregularities take place. Most station owners agree that the barter taking place in stations is small compared with what takes place at conventions.

When Joe Albritton bought the *Washington Star* and WMAL a few years ago, he was faced with a National Association of Broadcasters (NAB) ruling that he couldn't own both a radio station and a newspaper in the same area. If he sold the radio station immediately, he couldn't get as good a price. However, if the radio station appealed the ruling, taking the case to the Supreme Court, it could hold up the sale indefinitely, or even change the ruling. So a barter was struck. The station received an extension of five years from the NAB in return for not taking the case to court. The barter paid off and the station was sold in its own time frame for the highest price ever paid for any Washington station.

One of the most daring and imaginative barters took place in New Zealand some years back at a time when all radio stations were government-owned and -operated. A group of young men got the idea of placing a transmitter on a ship anchored 12 miles from shore. At the time, they didn't own a ship, but after approaching a shipowner worked out a deal. They would get the use of one of his ships free if after they got the government to agree to having the station on land, the shipowner could be on the board of directors. It looked like clear sailing until they discovered the Minister of Marine who granted harbor permits was also the Minister of Broadcasting. Figuring at that point they had nothing to lose, they went to him and discovered that he actually sympathized with their position, believing there should be privately owned stations. He gave them the permission they wanted, and promised that if they did a constructive job and the public pressured the government to change the policy permitting private broadcasting, he would not block the change. Two years later the government licensed the first commercial station, and the shipowner was appointed to its board.

A list of U.S. media brokers and sample of a broker's contract and ad follow:

List of some U.S. media brokers

Atwood Richards, Inc.
99 Park Ave.
New York, New York 10016

Corporate Image, Inc.
375 Park Ave.
New York, New York 10022

Mediators, Inc.
39 West 55th St.
New York, New York 10019

Video Enterprises, Inc. (specializing in game shows)
667 Madison Ave.
New York, New York 10021 or
8271 Sunset Blvd.
Los Angeles, California 90069

William B. Tanner, Inc.
2714 Union Ext.
Memphis, Tennessee 38112

SMY, Inc.
360 N. Michigan Ave.
Chicago, Illinois 60601

Promotional Services, Inc.
501 Madison Ave.
New York, New York 10022

Media Tours, Inc.
P.O. Box 14726
Las Vegas, Nevada 89114

Gamble Coker Advertising
P.O. Box 359
Boulder, Colorado 80302

Media Broker
625 Pacific Coast Highway
Santa Monica, California 90402

Courtesy Checks, Inc.
9011 Manchester Rd.
St. Louis, Missouri 63144

The American Association of Advertising Agencies issues an AAAA Directory of Media Buying Services. Write to 200 Park Ave., New York, New York 10017.

See also: Autos, Business of Barter, Public Relations and Promotion.

Sample Contract and Ad

MEDIA MAN, INC.

RECIPROCAL TRADE
MEDIA BROKER

1250 East Hallandale Beach Blvd.   Hallandale, Fl. 33009
BROWARD (305) 925-4800   DADE (305) 947-9929

CONTRACT NO._____

AGREEMENT made as of this _____ day of _____, 19___, between _____ (hereinafter called "the Station") and MEDIA MAN of Dania, Florida (hereinafter called "MM"):

AS FOLLOWS: The station hereby agrees to purchase from MM and MM hereby agrees to sell to the Station, the item(s) hereinafter described upon the conditions and terms hereinafter set forth:

1. MM agrees to sell to the Station, and the Station agrees to purchase from MM, the listed item(s), to be used within one year from above date, or as indicated.

2. In payment for the foregoing, the Station agrees to establish a credit in favor of MM as follows:

3. MM shall have the right to draw upon the said credit as a regular purchaser of time on behalf of its clients and their products excluding, however, Station's existing cash advertisers. It is understood that the time so purchased shall be pre-emptible for cash advertisers but that in the event of pre-emption, substitute availabilities within the same time classification will be offered in accordance with Station's current pre-emption policy.

4. The Agreement shall be binding upon the parties hereto and their assigns and successors in interests.

5. All clients or assignees shall be submitted to the Station for clearance. Station will not unreasonably withhold such clearance.

6. The Station agrees that at the end of each month it will furnish MM with detailed affidavits of performance covering the announcements used during the preceding month against the aforementioned credit.

MEDIA MAN by: _____

MEDIA by: _____

TITLE: _____

Sign and return original—keep yellow copy for your files.

Organizations

Tomorrow We'll Get Organized!

The fact that you belong to an organization means that you are a barterer. Organizations by their very existence are formed to trade information, collections, and assistance to one another, the community, or the world. In return for membership, time, and sometimes dues, your name is included on its rolls and you receive: a uniform if it has one, power by association, group or union benefits, discounts, social activities, personal affiliation, and help.

As an organization, a group amasses powerful trading cards to play in the outside world—reputation, good deeds, grants (to give as well as receive), and goodwill. Of these, goodwill is the least recognized by those who have it and the most sought after by those who need it. Politicians, educators, radio and TV personalities will speak to organizations free in return for goodwill (and publicity). Businesses donate space or merchandise for goodwill (and tax deductions). You can trade goodwill (depending on the size of your membership) for hotel rooms to host visiting speakers, out-of-town trips to conventions, meeting halls, or printing. Anything available to the donor at cost is available to your organization for goodwill.

For instance, if you have a large annual social event, you can get free publicity, printing, entertainment; prizes donated by celebrities; TVs, dinners, and cameras for door prizes; models and clothes for fashion shows (see Entertainment, Parties).

If historically or architecturally motivated, you can apply for and get architectural students or state employees to do surveys in return for room and board or office space. Many organizations are eligible for in-kind or matching funds that they never collect (check with county government offices; there is usually one specific staff member assigned to research such freebies). Or apply directly to state and national organizations whose goals are similar to yours. You can receive matching funds in return for providing office space, housing, consultation, or volunteered hours of your membership. If professionals (such as architects) help, you can claim their full hourly rate. Local colleges will supply students to help with research and clerical duties in return for educational credits. The National Guard will donate services of reservists to help with the work. If you've already finished the job, apply to one of the companies that give awards for community service (such as Bird & Son or Shell Oil) and get in line for money, awards, or recognition.

Want to build a clubhouse but don't have the land? National agencies can't sell federal land, but they can trade parcels they have to a worthy cause for a piece the same size. Once such a trade is arranged, find a philanthropist in the community to donate it in return for putting his name on your building.

Or you may find that the building you need is already built, unused, and owned by someone else. When a large builder ran into opposition in a farming community because of his tract development, he donated the historic tollhouse on the grounds to a local organization. In addition to reversing public sentiment, he also received a nice deduction on his tax bill.

Local welfare offices have special grants to employ needy persons. The government pays the salary of the worker and the agency then loans the services of the person to a local organization. Sometimes all an organization must do is submit a job description for approval. Other grants available to train unskilled unemployed workers will pay half his salary, allowing the remainder to be paid in matching funds or in-kind services. Go-between agencies are eager for organizations to apply for these grants but can't advertise the fact. Matching funds, a rich source of revenue, are sometimes used four times over to pay for rent and to hire help. If a matching grant of $1,000 comes through a community office in return for office space, a typewriter, and a secretary, this money can be used to apply against other matching grants. Since matched services do not have to be used full-time, they can be used as credits for other services or applied toward additional in-kind grants.

If an organization has a historic house, it can trade donated furnishings with other museums to obtain those of the period of the house. It can apply for and get aid from organizations with similar interests on a one-shot, regular, or long-term basis. And it can get a loan to buy a house from state historical organizations and pay off the loan by matching services or funds. If the site is of architectural or historical significance (such as Colonial Williamsburg), the organization can barter with manufacturers for the use of their name or patterns for furniture, fabric, or wallpaper and receive a percentage from all sales of items reproduced from its collection. A room of the house can be used as a community museum to obtain and keep collections in the community. If important collections have already left the area for national museums, other items can be used as barter to get them back. In 1971 the Delaware National Guard traded a 1793 Spanish bronze 9-pounder gun to the National Park Service for an Austrian 6-pounder field gun, then flew its gun to its new home at San Juan National Historical Park in Puerto Rico in a training exercise. Two years later the Dayton, Ohio, Veterans Administration traded two Civil War mortars to the Park Service for Petersburg National Military Park in return for two 12-pounder field guns.

If an organization needs additional funds, it can use a room as a consignment shop, borrow merchandise from consignors, and sell it in return for collecting 10 to 50 percent of the selling price (or 100 percent if it's donated). As a shopowner, it is eligible to obtain a sales tax number, allowing it to buy wholesale from dealers or at lower prices at auction (because the tax is paid by the buyer when it is later resold). If your organization frequently needs legal advice, you can (with permission of the zoning board) trade free rent to a lawyer for his services; or if you save and restore old houses, offer an office on the same terms to a plumber, electrician, or realtor. If you work with children's groups, you may be eligible to receive free sports equipment, a baseball diamond, tickets to events, or even a complete circus. If you have a protected, climatized environment, other museums and sites will loan you collections to house while their buildings are being renovated.

If your organization needs an approved kitchen to host fundraising dinners, work out a trade with local volunteer groups or church auxiliary to go fifty-fifty on costs in return for sharing the facilities (especially a downtown location). Need curtains? Ask the local extension group or sewing circle to make them in return for holding monthly meetings on the premises. Publicity? Give an annual award for good deeds in the community, getting local businesses to pay the bills for having their names associated with the venture. Or give an award to a celebrity and insist that he come to your hometown to receive it. Money? Have a ball on the premises and reward ticket sellers with a percentage of tickets.

Does your parent organization give grants or scholarships to local institutions or colleges ("local" meaning anything within 100 miles)? Insist that they be made through your branch. In addition to publicity—a major brownie point—you may receive help from the recipient organization, use of their facilities, speakers, and special invitations, which you can use or trade for other things.

What's the consuming passion in your community? If it's sports, sponsor an event at the local country club, trading the work of your membership in return for publicity, the club's name on the trophy, and free tickets. House tours? Borrow a model home from a builder, and ask local designers and decorators each to furnish a room. Let the builder pay moving charges and advertising; the decorators loan the furniture; while your organization collects admissions in return for putting the whole thing together (good publicity for everyone involved).

In addition to getting, look through your inventories to see what you can give or share. Fire companies can loan use of an existing kitchen to the extension ladies in return for their help at suppers. A sportsmen's club can give lessons or use of facilities to a scout troop in return for regular help with the maintenance.

Then take stock of all the expertise your group has to offer. A garden club can trade gardening lessons for speakers, judges, or flowers. The League of Women Voters can offer an internship to a college student who gains experience while doing the organization's work. Washington Independent Writers gave two journalism students the opportunity to produce its monthly newsletter. The students received experience and credentials; the club got free editorial help with the newsletter. You can get students in a profession to practice skills within your organization (such as a dental clinic for needy children, or archeological digs at a historic site).

Others are delighted to do bookkeeping or telephoning in return for free membership.

In addition to having more clout to barter outside the group, large organizations have more members available for bartering within. One of the best means of communicating and matching needs is a newsletter. Parents Without Partners, for instance, has swap columns which frequently find a newly separated man to fix appliances for a widow in return for home-cooked meals (such barters have been known to escalate).

Once an organization becomes a bureaucracy, barter may be the only way to get around dead ends. A major university shifted offices, resulting in one department having more furniture than space. The department could not get authorization to sell or junk the furniture, which belonged to the university and not the department; however, it could be traded off within the institution. One clear-headed member bartered the furniture to the university's computer center in return for $3,500 worth of computer time which the department couldn't afford in its budget. Since the computer wasn't being used full-time, everybody won, including the university.

Each year at international jamborees, the Boy Scouts of America enjoy a very personal form of barter through "patch swapping." Trading patches with other scouts has expanded over the years into stamp collecting, exchanging berets, and pen-pal relationships, often leading to exchanged visits in each other's country. In all the exchanges, ground rules are set by the swappers; but the most important trading card among the scouts, and the glue that makes most organizations stick remains the same—friendship.

Parties

Let's Have a Party (I'll Bring the Guests)

Elsa Maxwell, one of the world's most creative hostesses (George Bernard Shaw called her the eighth wonder of the world), gave her first party for twelve people for a total of $7. Forty years later she was treating 1,000 children to the circus at Madison Square Garden annually and it didn't cost her a cent. The *Journal American* and Pepsi Cola Company co-hosted the affair, John Ringling North paid for the tickets, and the police department provided the transportation.

For her April in Paris Ball each year, large textile firms contributed as much as 25,000 yards of luxury materials, famous artists entertained without charge, and debutantes served as models in the style show. People knocked each other down to pay $150 for tickets because not only was it an "in" affair but almost everyone took home a prize. Elsa got companies to donate autos, TV sets, furs, and jewelry as raffle prizes.

There are lots of ways to give parties without money. How? Well, if you're already famous, you can be a continual guest of honor and let others pick up the tab. If you're not, decide where you would like to entertain, make the arrangements through whoever is in charge, invite the guests—and tell them to bring their own refreshments.

David Bork, president of CODA Corporation, has an annual kite fly-in on the Antietam Battlefield during the Easter season. Friends and families come all day lugging baskets of food and homemade kites, vying for token prizes for the smallest, largest, most colorful, and highest flying models. David sends out the invitations, and the guests (with the cooperation of the weather) pro-

132

vide the entertainment. Never one to aim low, David has also hit upon a smashing, inexpensive alternative to after-theater entertaining. Packing crystal goblets, napkins, wine, and cheese in a picnic basket, he invites one or two couples to join him on his favorite park bench in Lafayette Square, facing the White House, where the entertainment is guessing what's going on inside the Big House. Rumor has it that at least one novel was born during these soirees.

Something that few can resist is going someplace they have never been before (preferably free for the asking). Let the refreshments and entertainment be dictated by the location, and then go en masse to the bottom of a mineshaft or the top of a belltower, to a winery or brewery; or how about a mystery trip? Barter for bus transportation if it's a large group and go to an undisclosed destination, such as a ballet studio where a teacher is waiting to give your guests a free lesson. One writer took a select group of friends up for a free balloon ride as a side barter to researching an article on the subject. Membership in a Cub Scout troop zoomed after parties were planned around two informal trips: one to a karate studio, the other behind scenes at Houston's Astrodome before it was opened to the public. Isn't there someplace in your community that everyone wonders about but no one has been to, such as the top of a firetower? Inside a radio station? Find out who is in charge and make arrangements (they'll see it as good public relations and/or publicity). Another version of the bring-your-own is the ad-lib party. Ask each guest to bring a costume or clothing for someone else to wear. After the guests arrive, each works out his or her own barter. Once negotiations are completed, each person must then spend the evening talking and acting like the character he or she represents. Or reserve the entire audience of a local TV show. See the producer or director beforehand, check his calendar to see which future program interests you, then tell him you will provide the cheering section.

Always wanted a birthday party? Give gifts or favors to friends on their birthdays and about one month before yours, tell each of them that you've never had a birthday party.

If you know a politician, tell him you'll host a party if he will pay for refreshments. Provide a service for a friend in return for his giving you a party to celebrate completion: like decorating his apartment, planting an herb garden, or painting one of his rooms.

One party giver, after a disastrous house fire, worked out a barter with her insurance man in return for two free parties. The first centered on a game of guessing the identity of burned objects; the second celebrated the restoration of the damaged property. She provided the preparation and sent out the invitations. Her insurance man paid the bill, increased present coverage for almost everyone there, and sold additional policies.

Trade a party for a party. Invite as many couples as your home can handle, suggest a gourmet club, and take turns giving parties monthly. Some clubs become elaborate, with international meals, printed recipes, and costumes. If you are far from home, groups can get together to celebrate each other's birthdays or trade celebrations, having Thanksgiving at one member's home, the Fourth of July at another—a dozen parties for the price of one. Pot-luck suppers are simple barters: you eat my casserole, I eat your brownies. It's easy entertaining all around . . . as long as someone coordinates each meal so that the buffet doesn't become variations on a lasagne theme. Leave it to the host to provide the least transportable food. If you live in a neighborhood where pot-luck suppers are the regular bill of fare, make yours more imaginative: all vegetarian, or only old family recipes, or finger foods. Have a soup party or a dessert tasting. Try a wine-and-cheese sampler, or if you're more ambitious, a hunt breakfast (you don't need horses).

Progressive dinners are another form of party barter in which each guest hosts one course. But if all the homes are not within walking distance, you may find this a diabolical make-work project that costs more than the sum of its parts (unless it takes place in summer yards). You have to coordinate transportation; hosts for the next course often have to get a head start on the crowd to finish last-minute preparations, or stay afterward for cleanup.

More efficient is a barter party, in which everyone contributes what he or she does best. The one with the largest home—you guessed it—is the host (unless there is a person who particularly enjoys cleaning house). Let the person with the most interesting acquaintances invite the guests, or suggest that each person invite three new people. Include someone who plays the guitar or piano.

Other assets to the crowd: a florist or baker, an undertaker (he has extra chairs), and, of course, the best cooks in town.

A side benefit of regular group parties is that each one can invest in special equipment and trade off with everyone else. One neighbor may have three dozen snack plates, or two neighbors can buy the same pattern and combine them. A case of wineglasses, a fifty-cup coffee maker, a large supply of coffee cups—the possibilities are endless.

Large liquor stores often provide wine at cost to groups or organizations, as well as a free film and someone to lecture on wines. The group spends three or four hours sampling different wines; the shopowner usually provides literature or cards describing the region and characteristics of each. Social or fraternal clubs have discovered that this is an ideal way to gain a captive audience for club dinners. The shopowner chalks it up as advertising to bring new customers into his store, while the organization has an opportunity to make a profit on the wine it buys at cost.

If you prefer hosting a party, you can maneuver all kinds of free help. The newest caterer in town might do it at cost (or for free) if you promise to invite party givers to sample his food. A food supplier might donate hors d'oeuvres in return for publicity, or some of your hand-thrown pots, a regular supply of flowers from your garden, or even the use of your house for other parties. If you need help serving or cleaning up, trade cooking lessons, a coveted introduction or invitation, or the use of your piano to a neighborhood teen-ager in return for his assistance. If you prepare your own food, make double batches, trading off half with a friend in return for his specialty. If you love to make Christmas cookies but can never find time to make all the variations you'd like, invite friends in for a bake-off, or bake separately, getting together afterward to swap varieties and recipes over tea.

Persuade a local organization to give an award. Have the presentation made at your house at a party (with the committee picking up the tab), or if you want to go first class, select the nicest club in town; or after a successful fund-raising event, suggest a celebration at your house and let the organization pay the bill.

Alternatively, get an organization to sponsor a celebrity auction as a fund-raiser. Gather up unusual things that will gain good bids and publicity (not to mention a great time), such as having the mayor read a bedtime story or the librarian dancing a hula; or a lock of hair from the baldest man in town.

TV and radio stations traditionally give glamorous parties but seldom pay for them in cash. They trade advertising time for cocktail parties, meals, bar privileges, paying the bill with air time that would otherwise be lost (or, as they say in the trade, "dead time"). The caterer or restaurant providing the food gains media time and a valuable showcase for the product, as well as contacts among the very people needed for future publicity and business.

Publicity is a highly barterable commodity. If your party is hosting a movie star or governor, everything from limousine service to canapés is available once you make it known to the appropriate source.

Charity benefits have two cases to make: the potential publicity and tax deductions. Businesses will donate flowers, food, entertainment, speakers, and raffle or auction prizes for the chance to take a deduction, and they do so eagerly if their name is clearly associated with donations.

Or take another leaf out of Elsa's book. She once hosted a celebrity cook-off at Romanoff's and invited stars such as Claudette Colbert, Clark Gable, and Ronald Coleman as the entertainment. If you can't arrange that kind of star billing, get local food writers to star, or have the husbands do the cooking at the next mother-and-daughter banquet. By doing what no one else has thought of, or rearranging what is already being done, everyone will want to come, someone else will be doing the work and paying the bills, while you will be having all the fun.

See also: Food, Organizations.

Professionals

An Eye for an Eye:
How to Barter for Professional Services,
or a Tooth for a...?

Nobody knows exactly why, but dentists win hands down as the most prolific barterers. Two Washington, D.C., dentists have covered their walls with art obtained through barter (in one instance for a capped tooth inlaid with a silver star in honor of the Bicentennial). Each dentist has devised his own barter principles. One barters only for luxuries (or, as he calls them, stolen pleasures). Some barter for services (motorcycle repair, carpentry); others barter only for tangible goods, preferring not to have to compare the price of an hour's worth of dentistry with an hour of plumbing.

Six suits, a two-year supply of wine, champagne—these are just the beginning of what one dentist bartered. "I feel the patient out before I make an offer," he explained, "to make sure he has something I really want," before he trades $100 worth of work for $100 worth of merchandise (wholesale, that is). And, to be fair, he gives barter and cash patients equal treatment in terms of scheduling.

Professional barter is so lucrative it encourages people to join the profession. How many potential medical students have been lured by the thought of free medical care for life? If doctors aren't halfway there as barterers when they get their degree, a month on the job will convince them. Drug companies include swap columns in the newsletters they send. Free samples arrive daily in the mail with encouragements that doctors prescribe them. It is unheard of for a doctor to have to buy his baby's formula or disposable diapers;

and have you ever seen a doctor's refrigerator or desk drawers that weren't stuffed with samples?

Medical swaps range from the pedestrian (the pediatrician cares for the veterinarian's children in return for medical aid for his pets) to the cosmic (many clergymen receive free medical care in return for their goodwill and prayers). If you contribute to the local rescue squad, you receive free medical training (which in turn will reduce your medical bills). Find a group that wants you (auto clubs, professional or union) and get rates 25 to 40 percent lower on your health insurance. If you have excess income this year that will push you into a higher bracket, pay the doctor and dentist bills for next year in advance.

One painter wrote us that her doctor was about to arrive in her studio to pick out a painting in exchange for her $80 medical bills. Obviously a prolific artist, she had already exchanged her artwork for legal services, hearing aids, optometry, and three new fenders for her car. She trades drawings to a newspaper for advertising space, art lessons for framing and matting, and this information to us for her name in this book. Thanks, Elizabeth Beer; we'll do business with you any time.

Many professionals trade services within their own profession. A lawyer who specializes in energy will trade information with a tax man. In addition to encouraging specialization, the arrangement also gives each the benefit of greater expertise.

Professional barters have a way of escalating. Carol Ridker, one of Washington's best-known potters, bartered on a regular basis with a young architecture student—her pots for his drawings. Eventually, as their respective professions developed, she traded him three valuable porcelain pots for his designing a new studio and house extension for her. She now has a spectacular studio. He has three works of art he could not afford, in addition to ever-widening publicity that comes from designing a structure that attracts acclaim.

Another architect started by designing quarters for a tax consultant in exchange for organizing the firm's books. As the tax consultant's business flourished, he began buying up properties for investment. The architect continued the relationship, renovating properties in exchange for accounting. Last we heard, the architect and tax consultant (cum real estate investor) had become full-fledged partners on the way to their first million.

Hardly a profession operates without some barter. Football players are traded in some of history's most public barters. Government agencies trade personnel, either from agency to agency or from state to state. Businesses lend employees to the government, or to public interest organizations.

Writers and editors depend on barter for many of life's expensive pleasures. One writer created a brochure for an airline in exchange for a round-trip fare, then did a repeat assignment for hotel room and meals. The editing of one doctoral dissertation, we learned firsthand, was worth a silver necklace, two silk scarves, six slipware plates, a bag of pears, two squashes, two urns, and a dozen long-stem yellow roses. One of us started a career as a restaurant critic for a small newspaper in exchange for its weekly dinner for two. It escalated into a full-time staff job as restaurant critic for the *Washington Post*. Writers also barter for necessities and often for office space in exchange for editing a newsletter, writing a column, ghosting political speeches, or even answering the phone.

Investigative writers needing case histories on alleged corruption, or information on social issues, privacy, computer data banks, medical records, credit, and so on, may obtain them free from certain data banks in return for feeding the system additional information.

Barter is involved in book fees and contracts. When the work of a celebrity (who is often paid more than professional writers) needs polishing, a writer is hired. If he has enough credits, he can barter to get his name on the cover ("as told to," or co-authorship) instead of accepting a straight fee and no credit line. One researcher, paid by the hour to dig out information for a book that developed into a best-seller, was shocked to see that 50 percent of the finished product was his research verbatim. If he had worked without pay for a percentage and bet on himself as co-author, he would now be a millionaire.

Another writer who had difficulty selling his book to a publisher asked a successful writer to look it over and tell him why. The top writer paid him $20,000 to run it through his typewriter and collect all remaining rights and profits. If the original author had held out for a fifty-fifty deal in profits as well as co-authorship, he would have fared better.

Most professional barters cost each party comparatively little in time and save much money. The biggest plus in most transactions is the fringe benefits. Anyone can have a pediatrician and pay a monthly bill. A barter relationship with a friendly pediatrician gives you a friend who won't get mad at you for calling when you are not sure the call is necessary. And the pediatrician who bartered with the veterinarian received a Christmas gift with the explanation, "My children were sicker than your dogs this year."

Knowing the electrician or plumber personally in a one-to-one barter frees you to call him when the toilet breaks on Sunday (and after he repairs it, to offer him a drink or dinner). From another point of view, each barter has the potential of bringing in a long-term client. Once a lawyer starts on your will or a dentist on your teeth, he will have your business for years, even after you become so successful that you must resort to cash. Some doctors and lawyers are careful to specify that they are not officially advising the recipient, in order to protect themselves from malpractice suits. But that need not stop you from acting on the free information.

And then there is the sentimental value of barter. One lawyer, in looking back on his legal cases after he retired, remembered most fondly the one he handled in exchange for a 4-pound loaf of rye bread.

Public Relations and Promotion

Barter in public relations and promotion can be as subtle as the selling of a presidential candidate or as obvious as green stamps. Although the subtle avoids the obvious, the obvious, in order to be effective, must use the tactics of the subtle to have a strong foundation.

Either, whether aimed at a single day or carried through a life-time of image building, can disintegrate with the wrong approach, inadequate research, a careless remark, the overdone grandstand play, or even a failure to say thank you.

If you think public relations doesn't involve you, think again. Understanding how it works can help you get a better job (by promoting yourself), build up attendance at the PTA, or even sell your house. What builds up sales in a billion-dollar corporation can also improve relationships over the backyard fence.

First, let's examine the subtle barter: implied but seldom stated, open-ended but never obvious; a delicate balance between the favor without strings and a whispered promise, it is much like a beauti-ful present left without a name tag in the middle of a table. The subtle approach informs all passers-by what is in the package, the date it can be opened and under what conditions, so that when the time comes, everyone wants to be there to see what's inside.

To demonstrate how this comes about, let's pretend your com-munity has decided to hold a craft fair. You want as many people each day as the fairgrounds can hold. You want to charge enough admission, but not so much that families will stay away, so you provide a built-in barter: children under twelve may attend free if with their parents, and free parking will be provided. You may work out a fifty-fifty deal with the fairgrounds or the local Jaycees to co-sponsor the event, building up the number of workers while cutting down expenses. You may also agree to share the wealth with local merchants by distributing their directory to craftsmen so that they can patronize local businesses while in town, or contract the food to volunteer organizations in return for a percentage of their profits. To involve a greater number of the community, and because newspapers often establish space quotas on how much publicity can be given an event, look for additional reasons for them to write about you (as well as lend additional voices to your promotional chorus). One way to do this is to provide free enter-tainment for local organizations—easily achieved by working up a slide presentation of the crafts to be shown and attending club meetings a few months before the event. Each time you provide a program, it can be written up in the paper (if not by them, by you). If you can find ways to involve each organization further, such as asking for overnight accommodations for the craftsmen in return for passes (not to mention that craftsmen pay their own way with crafts), you will gain more publicity while freeing motels for the visiting public. You can sometimes arrange free camping for the craftsmen at a local college or Y in return for arranging an educational program, which pays off in additional publicity each time a lecturer is announced, as well as after he speaks. Meanwhile you've decided who and where your audience is and started pulling them in from the outer fringes through other barters. If you decide yours is a family event, this means getting the names of editors and addresses of newspapers in a geographical radius within a day's driving distance.

Each time you do anything newsworthy, send out a release starting with the announcement. Papers always need news, but they won't print what you send them unless you find a way to *make* it news. If your event is the first of its kind, is of national importance, or will contain the greatest number of exhibitors ever shown in that region, it's news. The hometown newspapers of each craftsman will consider news of their acceptance, and if you plan on having an important celebrity attend the fair, that will become statewide news, if not national. If there's controversy over the affair and you can fan it while controlling the action, that's news to garner even more publicity. If ticket sales aren't moving, sell blocks of tickets to a well-located gas station to offer at half price or free with a fill-up, or start a campaign of letters to the editor about some aspect of the event. After you've listed priorities, determined the audience and geographical promotion area, done your research, and set up a timetable, a marvelous puzzle of pieces will start coming together from the outer edges, meeting at the center—the event.

Benefit previews of plays and exhibits are similarly planned but by inverse ratios. The fewer people who can attend, the more exclusive it is, the greater number will want tickets; therefore, the more you can charge. If it is by invitation only, the barters coming your way will be phenomenal, because everyone in business will want to be associated with the event. You will be able to barter for free programs, tickets, flowers, music, volunteers, decorations, and even limousine service for celebrities in return for free ads or mention. If it's going to become an annual event, sharing it with a good cause (such as a museum) will bring in additional publicity as well as adding its mailing list to yours. If you invite and obtain acceptance from celebrities, you can barter with the media for exclusive coverage. In this connection it pays to go to the top first, because if you let others in on the scoop, it will not be considered as a feature. TV channels work the same way. Most talk shows will barter an appearance in return for an exclusive or a promise that no other station will get it for three days. Therefore, to make the best barter, offer it to the highest-rated show first.

When a Baltimore television station discovered that Joan Mondale, wife of the vice-president, was going to attend the opening of the Winter Market of American Crafts, it realized it could go national on the network if it shot the event first. Unfortunately, the show was at noon and Mrs. Mondale's press conference was at 1:00 P.M. The only way the station could scoop the event was to interview her immediately after her entrance into the building at 11:00 A.M. Since she is a potter, the station decided a potter's wheel might do the trick. If a potter at a wheel could be placed just inside the entrance, the cameras would be there. The barter was struck. The wheel, potter, equipment, and clay—all found at different sources between midnight and 1:00 A.M. the previous night—were collected and picked up early the next morning. The setup worked . . . and looked natural as well.

If you can find a way to combine a celebrity with an unusual activity and know about it in advance, it can become national news without any effort at all. A good example of this happened recently in Washington, D.C., when the services of Elizabeth Taylor as cook and her husband, John Warner, as butler were offered as one of the attractions in a charity auction.

Another barter that happens regularly among publications and institutions is trading mailing lists. One way this is achieved is when a museum holds a special exhibit and an editor is invited as guest speaker or to receive a notable award. This is a multilayered barter because the publication will then feature the museum, the museum will obtain a free speaker, and each mailing list will grow. Another frequent trade-off is done annually by colleges granting honorary degrees at graduation to celebrities in return for their appearance, which in turn enhances their image and publicity.

In recent years department stores have found that gala openings for the benefit of a local cause or institution have the same effect. More often than not the institution selected for the honor has a mailing list of exactly the type of clientele the store would like to cultivate as customers. Movie and TV stars attend free in return for being featured in newspaper ads, if the book, movie, or cause they are touting is highlighted. If the star is a big draw, arrangements may be made to feature her in a fur ad to reimburse her for her efforts. The stores—if the opening is executed skillfully and attended by the "right" people—are welcomed into the community with open arms and receive free advertising in news and feature pages of local newspapers.

Obtaining celebrities is a barter game in itself, one that requires contacts. This is carefully cultivated through favors in advance and on a continuing basis. Some publicists keep detailed, up-to-date files on contacts, prospects, and clients, listing weaknesses, needs, tastes, friends, and even hobbies. For instance, if they know that a good contact collects owl figurines, each time they see one they will let him know. The recipient then owes a favor and will also remember the publicist's name the next time he calls (because he'll think he's getting more owls). For the publicist actually to buy the owl as a gift would be a mistake as it would have to be refused, could be interpreted as a bribe, and so kill the contact instantly.

Another area of favors involves passes. A skilled p.r. person makes sure enough passes are given to the right people, but never sufficient to saturate the market. Sent in the mail with a note saying, "Enjoy the show," passes don't put pressure on the relationship; but to ask in advance if a publication will cover the event is a faux pas because anyone in a position to grant such a request could not afford to be compromised.

Other favors include giving news tips to newsmen, or recommending them to magazine editors for lush assignments; arranging for a magazine to receive a lucrative advertising account from another client; arranging introductions or invitations to parties; passing on or sharing favors; appearing on talk shows when asked so that the door is open when you need to publicize an event; or donating services instead of money to influential committees and organizations to make additional contacts.

After Elsa Maxwell invited a publisher to a few galas, his secretary called to express his gratitude and tell Elsa that he had established a $5,000 credit at Cartier's as a small token of appreciation. Elsa called back and asked if she could use the money to retain Fritz Kreisler to play at one of her parties. In addition to providing marvelous publicity for the party, it was the ingredient necessary for her to meet George Bernard Shaw.

Other more subtle promotional barters include granting exclusive merchandising rights in a territory in return for advertising and highlighting the product throughout the store; endorsement of a product by a celebrity in return for a contribution to his pet charity; or arranging his selection as judge in a national contest. Housing developers barter decorating of a model home with a store or decorator in return for mutual advertising. Individuals sometimes barter influence or contributions to organizations in return for a place on the board, adding prestige to both.

Another promotional ball game involves selling books. If an editor can arrange for a book to be selected by a book club, it increases the price paid for the paperback rights. If a good price is secured for both, it puts more leverage into negotiating the movie contract, each parlay increasing the number of books printed as well as the profits.

Before obvious promotional barters (in the form of box tops, coupons, trading stamps, labels, giveaways, and rebates) are undertaken, the needs of the public are carefully studied and the resulting premium or prize is geared to meet them.

If the promotion game appeals to you but you lack the experience, barter your talent for a chance to play it. Volunteer to do publicity for a worthwhile cause such as the local Cancer Society, mental health association, or theater group. While you're bartering your time for experience, you'll learn how to make contacts, write press releases, and handle public information. You can then use your talents to barter for other goods and services or even start your own business.

Public relations and promotion provide a challenging arena for barter. If you enjoy being the middleman, can keep your involvement low key, let others take credit for crowds and profits, and remember to pay back favors, keeping the momentum building upward and outward, your influence as well as your credit will grow.

And although good public relations as well as those masterminding it should never show, you will feel the good vibrations coming back a thousandfold each time you accomplish a coup. With a smile on your face, funneling people toward good times and products you recommend, always searching for the right combination or idea, your life will become as open-ended as your barters, and the world will want to help you open the present.

See also: Business of Barter, Fame, Media.

Sex

Lend a Hand and Take It from There

It has been said that George Bernard Shaw, upon meeting a lovely young thing at a cocktail party, asked if she would go to bed with him for $5 million. After she had agreed, he asked, "How about five dollars?" "What do you think I am," she asked, "a whore?" "We've already established that," he replied. "Now I'm trying to set the price."

If you are a beginner in barter, or a novice in sex, bartering sex may not be the best place to gain experience in either field. Despite the fact that sexual barters have been going on in varying degrees since Adam traded his rib for a wife in the Garden of Eden, the psychological, ethical, social, and moral overtones present in every stage of play, both mentally and physically, are charged with a dynamism that can X-rate your life when you least expect it long after you think you have forgotten the exchange.

As the George Bernard Shaw anecdote so aptly illustrates, sex means different things to different people. The many nuances of the term, plus mental images the word conjures when coupled with love, lust, marriage, status, honor, tradition, and/or procreation, are so intertwined throughout historical barters that it is often difficult to determine where one ends and the other begins.

Assuming that you know what barter entails, perhaps we should examine the word *sex*. Although the dictionary's first four definitions deal with the state of maleness and femaleness, relegating intercourse to fifth position, contemporary usage has a tendency to reverse the order and proportion, placing more emphasis on action and less on gender. For our purposes, we will discuss barter *of the individual* from historical to present times, including (for those of you who want to know) contemporary practices of what has come to be known as "the swinging set."

In the earliest forms of religion, humans as well as lambs and oxen were sacrificed as barter to the gods in atonement for sins or as payment for favors sought. To secure favorable results, the act had to be performed by the right person and in the right manner with no mistakes in detail.

In the give and take of barter since then, the exchange has included everything from kisses to countries. The innocent young women of fairy tales kissed frogs to win princes and promised infants for spun gold, objects, or brave deeds. The hero of "The Giant with the Three Golden Hairs" had to remove three golden hairs from the giant for the right to keep the bride. In Grimms' "Household Tales" a marriage was arranged in return for a branch of silver leaves and golden fruit, and in "Boots and His Brothers" the princess and half the kingdom were traded for felling an oak tree and digging a well.

Unlike fairy tales, in which love and marriage are interchangeable and usually arrive in that order, with sex presumed, history has a way of rearranging the deck, sometimes dealing from the bottom. As Mr. Shaw's conversation proved, the dice may also be loaded, and happy endings, although alluded to, are seldom guaranteed.

Barters also formed the basis for much of the action in Greek myths and tragedies. When Helen, the daughter of Zeus and wife of Menelaus, king of Sparta, was abducted by (or eloped with, depending on which version you read) Paris, son of the king of Troy, she set off the Trojan War and became "the face that launched a thousand ships." Unfortunately, the ships loaded with

Spartan troops couldn't sail for lack of wind. So Agamemnon (her husband's brother, who had taken charge of the troops), in one of the most dastardly barters of all time, sacrificed his daughter to the gods in return for the needed winds.

In those days barter was not only a way of life but often a means of keeping it. As soon as one side won a battle, they killed the men (so they would not live to fight another day) and took the women captive. The less beautiful or influential were bartered as slaves, and the more desirable could be traded as part of the peace terms or fought over, causing new battles. Toward the end of the war, when Agamemnon fell out with Achilles over possession of a captive maid, Briseis, Achilles withdrew his aid from battle. The war was eventually won when the Greeks persuaded the Trojans to take a horseful of soldiers. Once inside the city walls, the Greeks killed the men, took the women captive, and started an expression that has lasted to this day: "Never look a gift horse in the mouth"—good advice for anyone contemplating sexual barter.

In order to win the throne, Jason had to retrieve the Golden Fleece. Medea, daughter of its possessor, revealed the secrets of guarding them to Jason and fled with it and him, slaying her half brother along the way. The barter soured when Jason divorced her to marry Creusa. To avenge the barter, Medea murdered Creusa as well as her two sons by Jason and returned home.

Throughout history marital barter has been serious business, never to be taken lightly. Tribes formed important alliances through marriage. Nonpayment of an agreed-upon dowry could make a marriage invalid and the children of the union illegitimate. In some South African tribes, extramarital sex can be legitimized by payment of the required number of cattle. Marriage barters sometimes involve a reciprocal exchange of goods between families, but in most instances payment is made by the groom or his family to the family of the bride in return for the marriage. Tribes traded brides for cowrie shells, tobacco, feathers, and even jars. When the bartering of brides extended beyond regional borders, international trade was born with currencies determined by the value of a woman.

The Greek *prioka,* or dowry, consisting of anything from a herd of goats to a village olive grove, has been the backbone of Greek marriages for centuries, entrenched by thirty-two civil code articles under which daughters may sue fathers who refuse to provide the gift, and husbands may divorce their wives if they feel they were not the real beneficiaries in the marital contract.

Since pinching has been outlawed in Italy, merchants have been known to give healthy discounts to attractive females for pinching privileges. In other countries politicians have been toppled by disclosures of past or present sexual barters, and large corporations have been charged with providing prostitutes to visiting salesmen in return for contracts and favors. "Happy Hooker" Xaveria Hollander admitted she received monthly checks which she promptly returned to an architectural firm in exchange for being listed as a "consultant," in order to show legitimate income to cover up earnings from her "house."

Producers have been known to cast plays from couches; politicians have filled government slots with secretaries who can't type; and more than a few medical men have been charged by former patients who tired of "playing doctor" on examining tables in payment of the bill.

Barter in sex can be as subconscious as a wifely headache, as premeditated as a husband's invitation out to dinner to remove the headache, or as calculating as an immigrant marrying his way into another country or a mistress earning her keep. At least one Washington blonde has been known to pay her restaurant bills by signing her telephone number; power lovers who believe in strength by association sleep with high-ranking politicians in return for invitations, introductions, funding, or jobs. High school virgins give in to boy friends to keep the arrangement steady; girls become pregnant as barter toward marriage; showgirls shop at Tiffany's with credit cards belonging to sugar daddies—all forms of sexual barter.

Home-style sex started to elbow power elite escapades out of the news when housewives admitted to being call girls in return for more fun on the job or to obtain luxuries their budgets could not afford. Contemporary barter in sex began to spread. Although the public had long suspected that politicians were trading jobs for sex and sex for votes, suburbanites trading sex for lawn mowers made them believe that what money could not buy, sex probably could.

Magazines began describing mate-swapping parties where keys thrown in the middle of the floor decided which owners mated for the evening. After the year-round sport surfaced in California during the mid-1960s, sexual swingers began openly to develop a life-style and vocabulary all their own. Psychologists and social researchers have estimated that eight million Americans are now engaged in some form of swinging. Social clubs, nightclubs, organized parties at $10 to $20 a head (or bottom as the case may be), social clubs meeting at private homes, all became part of the bill of fare. Bars and restaurants sprang up in major cities where swingers could meet prospective partners, or have on-the-spot quickies in booths. Nationwide mailing services were set up for letter-swapping, with connections often completed by phone. Some thrill-seekers experimented first with nudist camps, and others plunged into swingers' clubs complete with mailing lists. After visiting other swingers, sometimes warming up with sexual encounter games, they branch out into encounters as singles or couples or participate in group gropes.

Those who want to trade sexual favors now have organizations and publications to satisfy their needs, once they pay the entrance fee or advertising rate. The Playmates International listing service in York, Pennsylvania, claims 10,000 coast-to-coast listings, with half from single men who have paid the $75 entry fee in the sexual sweepstakes. Because of the demand, single women and couples pay only $5. Applications have room for all kinds of options (individual or group activity, s/m, kinky sex), as well as a place to indicate willingness to travel or preference for home delivery. *Select Magazine*, published in Camden, New Jersey, one of more than 200 periodicals devoted to the swinging set, claims 5,000 subscribers and takes ads averaging $5 each from members who have already paid a $15 membership fee. A one-time ad costs 15¢ per word, and although women and couples can have their pictures published free, men must pay an additional $5 per photo. Issues carry as many as 4,000 barter classifieds. However, novices report discovering the hard way that "stewardesses" searching for "generous gents" or women desiring to "model" clothes are sometimes code words for prostitution. Mail-order flesh catalogs differ little from swinger magazines except that they are larger and slicker, with ad copy going into idiosyncrasies and sexual preferences. No restrictions are placed on such magazines as long as they don't send unsolicited material through the mail. Although the government has not interfered in these operations, they have not been accepted by major first-line distributors and are usually available only in adult bookstores.

Those who enjoy these exchanges—whether heterosexual or homosexual, paired or grouped—say that it is important to look on the activity as "pure sex," to keep it "without love" or "for experience only" in order to survive and be ready for the next liaison.

Bartering for sex is no game for amateurs. Even pros have been known to have problems in advance play that can prove irreversible. Before you start, make sure the terms of play are understood by both sides. Protect your bases by keeping alternatives available. If there is the slightest doubt in your mind, get terms in writing or you may become the bartered rather than the barterer.

Know in advance why you want to play. To relieve boredom? Get something you want? Act out your fantasies? Try to keep someone around? Get a free trip around the world? Or sex itself?

If sex is your only answer, perhaps you aren't asking yourself the right questions.

Sports and Equipment

Be a Sport

Trading baseball cards for other cards, marbles for better marbles, and box tops for basketballs is a way of life when we're young. But then (perhaps because money is such an ingrained habit in our society) we forget that trading is one of the more pleasant aspects of the game.

As soon as we start trading money, we use it as an excuse for not buying the sports equipment we want. When we're young, we're without it. As young adults we have too many necessary expenditures; middle age brings on the expenses of college tuition for our children or we feel guilty about indulging our cravings. If we wait until we can afford what we want, we're often too old to play.

For some of us, the greatest hurdle to bartering for sports and equipment is learning to consider them a necessity instead of a luxury.

Where do you start? Well, if you're a national sports figure, you can try for the top and get all the equipment you want by endorsing a product (but that type of barter is beyond the reach of most). Most sportsmen can't resist a good bet. Bet on yourself to win. Try some wagers with those you want to engage in trade.

Must your equipment be new, or can it be used? Do you need it full- or part-time? Do you want to own it or are you willing to settle for using, sharing, or borrowing someone else's? What do you have to trade? Once you find the answers, look around to see what someone else is not using that he might trade. If you're looking for sports equipment for your children, check out families whose children are older (you may find a permanent swapping partner). Older people whose noise tolerance level has decreased might even *pay* you to take their basketball net or tennis court equipment to your house. Once you find a likely prospect, make an offer.

If what you want is in a store, ask what the management will take in trade in services or time. He may need someone to mind the counter while he is on vacation, or take inventory, or keep the books. If you are skilled at a certain sport, offer to conduct Saturday morning classes up to the amount of your "purchase." (It may lead to more.) The smaller the store, the easier it will be to make a deal; but larger stores have more turnover in quantity and may have a job that no one else can find time to do (such as sharpening ice skates). Offer to collect overdue bills for 10 percent of what you get applied to your credit. If you own a store, offer part of your window display to advertise sports equipment.

If you decide equipment doesn't have to be new, check out local schools and athletic teams to be first in line when they replace old equipment with new. Trade telephoning to get what you want.

If you get a large quantity, trade it off to others. Summer camps are also good sources. Trade craft lessons or coaching for equipment; or tend the premises during winter months in return for using equipment all year. When a summer camp is going out of business, offer to take on the job of selling off its equipment in return for selecting what you want.

Check into the possibilities of being purchasing agent for community teams. Shop around for best prices and get your equipment free as commission from the company when you place the order.

Set up a local sports equipment exchange and get first choice. Or trade your time as manager for a percentage or selection. The Rippowan-Cisqua School in Bedford, New York, runs a Sport Swap each fall as fund-raiser. Parents and children bring unused sports equipment, each selling off and buying what they want with 40 percent of all sales going to the school.

If what you want is in a catalog, write to the company and ask what it'll take in trade. If it's direct mail, the company may accept names and addresses for its mailing list (usually fifteen names for each $1 credit). Or maybe it is looking for a local representative, who in addition to commission gets his own free sports equipment.

School personnel should check cereal boxes and soup cans in the school pantry. Kool-Aid offers money for empty K/A envelopes; Post Cereals, sports and playground equipment for box tops; Colgate, cash for proof of purchase on a number of household products; and Campbell's Soup, audio-visual and athletic equipment for labels.

Local sports clubs also have needs that can be translated into sports assets. If you don't have golf clubs, offer your services as a caddy. Learn while you earn, using the club's equipment and free golfing privileges. If you are more expert, maybe the club will let you give youngsters golfing lessons in return for the clubs you want from the shop. Check game, hunting, and archery club bulletin boards to see what trades are available. If the clubs need maintenance, perhaps they'll let you use their facilities free in return for labor, and throw in a membership too. Find out if you can get a membership at the Y in return for your services (telephoning, writing releases, or teaching classes).

If you're looking for a place to fish and hunt by yourself (rather than in a club), offer to help with the chores or repairs of a property in return for hunting privileges. Or, if you are the owner of a sports paradise and need help with the work, place an ad in the newspaper of the nearest town offering rights in return for help. But stand firm on ground rules. Insist hunters obey state and county game laws and advise you of the area in which they are hunting each day. Keep groups small for greater safety.

Like to ski? Offer to help with opening and closing a resort each season in return for a lift ticket. Or if you are an Olympic skier whose age demands a change in profession, offer advice on trail system layouts in return for free skiing for the family. It may become the experience necessary to becoming a full-time consultant.

Want a bike? Unlike car dealers, most cycle shopowners discourage trade-ins. "Trade-ins try to happen more often than they actually do," said one shopowner. Department store–type bikes are definitely not accepted because they are hard to guarantee. Appearance (paint and dirt) is not as important as sound mechanical condition, and "it's important to like the person," said one owner. "If I feel good about the person, he will get a more favorable deal." He has traded one bike for a skateboard, and another for legal services. Look around the shop to see what else it carries. One New York youngster who fell in love with a $62 model saw a sign for worms and bought his bike for 3,000 night crawlers.

Joe Richman is only twelve but, thanks to barter, has a busy skateboard repair shop in his basement. He traded two good skateboard wheels for four less-good wheels, plus pads, two old boards, and a few other parts. He sold one set of wheels for $13, the other for $8 (the original wheels cost $13), making $8 on the deal, and gaining parts to make and repair other boards. Before he made the trade, he figured who would buy the wheels and for how much. When someone gets new wheels, Joe will put them on free in exchange for the old wheels, which he sells or trades. He also trades finished skateboards for old ones, using the parts to make new skateboards.

Paul Ridker of Bethesda, Maryland, maintains a neighbor's tennis court in return for the privilege of using it, and he cleans pools on a regular basis for swimming. If there is a tennis club near you, it may be open to an offer of maintenance for lessons.

Or, if you are a professional (such as a psychiatrist), trade on an hour-for-hour basis.

If horseback riding is your thing, check out local stables and horse farms to see if they need help mending fences, cleaning stables, exercising, walking, or showing horses in return for riding free. Those with particular expertise in this field may be able to trade services for part ownership of a racehorse as well. Trading horses is much like trading used cars; each swap depends on the situation and the horses. If you find a horse you can't afford, sell shares. Once he starts winning, the breeding fee will pay off his purchase price in no time.

Do you hanker for a boat? Check local yacht clubs and dock space to find one not being used. Its owner may not be able to bring himself to sell it but because of health, money, or time may be no longer able to maintain it. Offer to help with the work in exchange for using it. If you do a good job and care about it as much as he does, he may give it to you and write it off as a tax deduction. Or perhaps it's not necessary to own a boat with all the headaches this entails. Offer to store a friend's boat for the winter in return for using it in the summer. If sailing is your game, check bulletin boards at yacht clubs to see who needs a crew. You don't always need experience to be selected. If you have other talents, such as cooking or sail-mending, or even if you are the right weight, you might win a berth.

Like to fish? Offer your labor on a fishing boat for a free ride, and get food for the table as well. If you end up with a surplus, swap it to the local tackle shop for fishing gear. Trade it with friends for other goods or services. With experience, you may soon own your own boat and be trading rides for others' services.

In any trade of sports equipment, check current prices to make sure you are getting a good deal. If the equipment is used, compare the cost of repair, add it to the age, and determine if it's really a bargain. Some items, such as snowmobiles, lose value through disuse and may not be worth a fraction of their original price. Ask for a time guarantee to ensure operation; get it in writing. For the best barter bargains, look for sports equipment where it is not normally used (for example, skis owned by a Florida ex-skier who has used them only once).

Sometimes the best deal, if it comes at the wrong time, is no deal at all. Recently, one of the players from the local high school came by to ask one of us if she would loan them her house for a cast party because all the other parents had turned them down. "No," she replied, "we've already had three cast parties, and that's enough."

"Try barter," Connie's son prompted the young thespian.

"What if we guarantee you thirty free workers to work around the property the day after the party?" Connie could feel herself weakening. Thirty workers *before* the party would be better, but it was too late for that.

"It's Sue's birthday anyway," another son reminded her. "We're having our own party that night."

After the young man left, Connie's son said, "Did you know his family owns the tennis club?" Lightbulbs flashed on in her head.

"Tennis lessons!" she gasped. "Now why didn't I think of that?"

Moral: Never stop hitting the ball back into the other guy's court until you're sure the game is over.

Taxes

"The art of taxation consists in so plucking the goose as to obtain the largest amount of feathers with the least possible amount of hissing."
—ascribed to J. B. Colbert, ca. 1665

You may not see yourself as a goose, but in 1975 approximately one out of three families paid more taxes than necessary, while eleven of the leading corporations in the United States paid no federal income tax.

Why? In addition to having capable tax lawyers to do their homework, and lobbyists skilled in the fine art of hissing, corporations realize savings through tax laws that provide incentives for engaging in various activities.

While the average individual does not enjoy similar tax benefits, if you arrange your income and outgo, keep accurate records, avail yourself of adequate advice, and learn to put the right asset in the proper pocket, you also may be able to reduce your taxes. This chapter touches on many of the ways this is accomplished. If you recognize one that describes your situation, investigate it further. Do your own homework and consult your tax adviser. You can also get free information by calling the IRS, but be prepared: if you call ten times, you may get ten different answers, as many decisions governing barter are still up in the air.

Because of the heightened interest and action in barter between both individuals and corporations, the IRS has in recent years looked with a wary eye on all such transactions. Although no money is actually exchanged, the exchange of services or goods at a fair market value represents income to both parties and therefore must be reported as income and taxed. However, many barters are deductible as business expenses.

For instance, if a decorator pays her $500 medical bill by decorating the dentist's office, she can deduct it as a medical expense while the dentist may be able to deduct part of her decorating as a professional expense with the rest of her fee added to the cost of the new furnishings and subject to depreciation in following years. To keep records straight, the IRS prefers that both parties write a letter stating the nature and amount of the barter, filing each as a paid bill. A current market price should be established for each item or service bartered with income declared for money, goods, or services received. The pertinent point in figuring taxes on barter is not how much you traded, but the fair market value of what you got in exchange.

If you obtain a car listed in the blue book for $3,000 in return for an antique car that you put together from parts, the antique car is worth the blue book value of the car received in exchange. Thus if you buy an old car for $300, then fix it up, expending $1,000 for parts, so that it is worth $3,000, at which time it is swapped for another car worth $3,000, the taxable amount of $1,700 is determined by taking the original $300 investment, adding the cost of your parts ($1,000), and subtracting the total from $3,000.

What matters as far as the IRS is concerned is intent. If an investor buys a farm intending to make a profit and does not (because of inexperience, weather, or finances), it is viewed as an honest mistake. The penalty comes when the IRS does not regard the venture as a true trade or business.

The IRS is more concerned with individuals trying to avoid paying taxes on income rather than making errors on deductions. While they tend to ignore small and informational barters, they are concerned about company or business barters engineered for tax purposes.

Trading property is more discoverable and therefore more vulnerable to question than trading services, yet realtors trade off properties on a regular basis to reap advantages of depreciation (see Land, Real Estate, and Mineral Rights chapter). Realtors dealing in rental properties usually keep them until their depreciation is used up, then trade them off for similar "in kind" properties owned by other realtors. It stands to reason that traded properties cannot always be of equal value, but a lesser property is considered more valuable if it is heavily mortgaged, since it may permit the realtor to claim depreciation all over again on the newly acquired property.

For businesses, tax benefits come in bartering when there is no appreciable financial gain and the resulting exchange benefits the company. If you trade a typewriter you don't need for a calculator you do need, no tax is paid but an excess asset is eliminated and a valuable one gained.

Section 1031 of the Internal Revenue Code states that there is no gain or loss recognized on a business trade of like kind property (not including inventory). Thus, if your business trades a typewriter for another typewriter, you don't have to pay taxes on the gain even when you get the better deal, unless you are a typewriter dealer and it is inventory. Likewise, if you could swap a New Orleans motel for a Seattle motel or an apartment building in Connecticut for one in Texas, you declare neither profit nor loss on the trade. The one criterion is that the properties must be like properties. The Code goes so far as to specify that trading livestock of different sexes does not fall under this rule. If you sell off one item in order to buy another, you must pay taxes on the gain; but if you barter like for like, you do not.

There are some special provisions for some items such as houses, but rules governing barter are in the statutes under "sale or exchange." Income, for taxable purposes, does not include gifts or inheritances, but if the IRS discovers that something has been made to appear as a gift when it is actually a barter, they will be displeased. However, there is a distinct difference between tax avoidance and tax evasion, a fine line that has enabled many individuals to become millionaires by taking advantage of special tax shelters in oil, farming, and real estate.

In recent years, many doctors and dentists have formed private corporations in order to realize tax savings. All money received for the services of the doctor or dentist goes into the corporation, a tax shelter consisting of many pockets, some of which are taxable and others not. The corporation adopts pension and profit-sharing plans, as well as pays fringe benefits. The income earned by the retirement funds is not subject to tax in the years it is earned; contributions to the retirement plans (25 percent of salary or $28,000, whichever is less) are deductible to the corporation when made and not taxable to the doctor or dentist at that time (but only later when he is actually paid, after he has retired and is in a lower tax bracket). The retirement fund can make investments on its own, earning additional income which is not taxed. The corporation then pays the doctor a salary, which is considerably less than his total earnings.

A retired individual who needs to increase his interest income because of a higher cost of living would have to pay capital gains if he sold mature stocks and bonds in order to reinvest in those paying a higher yield. But if he signs over his investments to a tax-exempt foundation (such as Colonial Williamsburg) or the college of his choice, donating them in a lifetime unitrust, the organization can sell them, reinvest in bonds paying more interest, sometimes increasing interest from 2 percent to 7 percent, which is paid to him for the rest of his life. At the time of the donor's death the securities revert to the institution or organization. If he has amassed a prized collection of furniture and wants to make sure it remains intact rather than being sold off after his death, he can donate it to a public charity or museum, give his house as well, and sometimes live in the house with his collection until his death, with expenses paid by the organization. If he first sold his property, the high capital gains might require that he sell his collection to pay the taxes.

There is a gamble implied in these transactions: the institution is betting that the individual will live a short time, reducing the amount of its investment; whereas the individual often feels that he will live longer once relieved of the financial and emotional burden of worrying over his assets.

How terms are arrived at depends to a great extent on who the individual is, how rare the collection is, how much the organization needs the property, the scope of the organization's finances, and what benefits exist for each party. If the person is a famous author whose papers would be a valuable asset to the college library, attracting additional funds or prestige, or if the residence is close enough to the campus to be converted into a museum or dormitory, the terms of the trade could be very generous. The income of the individual might determine whether he preferred to use the transaction as a charitable deduction or have it converted into an annuity (because a charitable deduction is allowed for the house but not the personal property if the individual retains an interest). If the person continues to live in the house with expenses paid by the beneficiary, he would have to declare total expenses paid as income. Parents who list their children as co-owners in return for lifetime tenancy must also list expenses as income if they are paid by the children.

Even if your house, property, or collection is not historically important or significant, it can be donated to an educational or religious organization during your lifetime through similar barter arrangements. In return for the remainder of your interest in a house you are given an annuity. You receive a guaranteed income for the rest of your life and on your death the entire estate belongs to the institution. If the estate is fairly large, the institution may even name a building in your honor during your lifetime and give you the added satisfaction of seeing your name up in stone.

Or perhaps you prefer to keep what you have in your own name. For example, assume that some years ago you invested in a painting for $10,000 which is now worth $100,000. If you keep it in your home, the cost of insurance is prohibitive and the chance of your home being robbed is increased. If you sell it, you will have to pay a capital gains tax on the $90,000 difference. But if you can work out an arrangement with an individual or institution at $10,000 a year plus interest for ten years, or $5,000 a year for life, the painting can help maintain your standard of living.

Some museums have discovered that they can add to their collections by offering to make a reproduction of an important piece of jewelry, furniture, or painting, then trade it to the owner for the original. In addition to the tax benefits involved, the owner has the assurance that an important piece will be in a safe, climatized environment. Generally, depending on an individual's overall income, he would be further ahead if he traded the original piece to the museum in exchange for a reproduction that has been made by the museum at its own expense. The amount of charitable deduction would be the difference between the value of the original and the cost of the reproduction.

When you want to give away what you don't want or need, getting the highest appraisal will give you a larger deduction. For instance, take a painting to a museum specialist rather than an antique dealer who may be appraising the value of the frame and not be as knowledgeable in the field of art. Some museums have been known to form special tax deduction cliques so that generous patrons can derive tax benefits in return for loaning the museum the money to buy art from the collection. When the museum decides on an acquisition, it arranges for the donor to pay as little as possible to obtain it, lets it "visit" the donor's home for at least a year, then appraises it for the highest amount possible (sometimes generated by a special one-man show in its own gallery). Some individuals arrange this buy-wholesale-sell-retail deal with two museums, buying as many as ten works of art by a given artist, publicizing the collection, then giving five works to each institution. If you wish to donate appreciated stock to a favorite charity, it may be better to donate it directly at the current value rather than selling it first, primarily because a capital gains tax is payable on the difference between the selling price and your original purchase price.

Another way to barter in taxes is to defer income. Since money is taxed only after it is received, individuals in high-income brackets (or on the verge of entering a higher bracket) go to great lengths to delay receipt of income. They also barter time, space, bookkeeping, and services to keep income down. Some professionals request fringe benefits from employers instead of raises, such as use of a company car, medical or group term insurance, or arranging for loans rather than taking advances for expenses (then charging off expenses against it until the amount is used up).

If you expect a high-income year, take advance deductions, paying church pledges and dental bills as well as real estate taxes for the coming year. It may also be possible to defer receipt of part of your income by postponing commissions and royalties until the following year or bunching deductions. Many companies don't mail dividends until December 31 so that they will not be received and therefore not taxed until the following year.

If your income is more than 20 percent greater than usual, and if the excess above 20 percent is at least $3,000, income-averaging will also save tax dollars. Your tax adviser can tell you additional ways to alleviate the tax burden by making gifts and bequests to your family; or investing in state, city, and municipal bonds that pay tax-free interest; or writing your will so that your heirs pay the least inheritance tax.

Some U.S. towns allow you to work off part of your municipal tax bill by bartering your labor or services. In others, if a property owner agrees to keep the road in front of his house free of snow or takes on maintenance of a park (mowing it regularly and keeping it free of glass), he does not have to pay city taxes. (However, the amount of taxes he saves may be income and therefore taxable by the state and federal governments.) In other communities, citizens pitch in to do the work instead of hiring municipal employees and raising their taxes. Middletown, Maryland, citizens build, clean, and repair their own sidewalks and contract for water and sewer maintenance, eliminating the need for full-time maintenance employees, and thus higher taxes. If you are an artist and your income does not meet your outgo, you might consider moving to Ireland, whose government does not tax artists.

Or, if you don't use part of your house or property, or spend only part of the year at a vacation home, you might consider becoming a landlord, gaining additional income which can be balanced out through depreciation allowed on rental property. If you own more than one house and plan to sell the one you are not living in, try to move into it first and establish that it has become your principal residence. The moving expense may be small compared with what you save in capital gains, which don't have to be paid on the sale if the property is the principal residence and proceeds are reinvested in another house within eighteen months before or after the sale. You can continue doing this on a regular basis until you turn sixty-five, building up equity as you go, provided that you can establish in each case that the house sold was your principal residence. After that, there is total or partial exclusion of capital gains.

If your job requires being available for emergency service (police, fire, repair, ambulance, newspaper) you can deduct part of your home telephone bills as ordinary and necessary expense of employment. Although you can't deduct commuting costs, you can deduct transportation to a second job and back again (but not home). You can also deduct transportation to solicit business, gain business information, collect bills, conduct interviews, visit patients, call on suppliers, use library or legal files, entertain customers, and inspect property sold, bought, or remodeled. If you use your car for business purposes, you can deduct either the standard mileage allowance (plus parking and tolls) or the actual cost of operating the car for business transportation. The latter deduction may be preferable if your car gets poor gas mileage.

If you are going abroad, check U.S. customs regulations to find ways to save on taxes, such as bringing back unstrung pearls (5 percent duty compared to 55 percent if they are strung), or buying a foreign car overseas, using it for traveling on vacation and importing it as a used car.

Ex-wives sometimes barter information on ex-husband's tax evasion practices in return for a percentage of what the IRS gains. But if the return was a joint return, this barter could backfire.

In recent years, women unable to go outside the home to work have found that swapping chores they don't like for those they do makes household tasks easier. Some also swap checks at the end of each week. By paying each other the same amount, the checks cancel each other out, while the barterers rack up experience, references, and Social Security benefits (not to mention increased self-esteem). However, if the husbands are in a high-income tax bracket, this additional "income" could push the family into an even higher bracket, increasing taxes and decreasing savings.

If you incur education expenses to maintain or improve skills, to comply with a local law or regulation for your present job or professional status, they can also be deducted. If you are a teacher, overseas travel directly related to your field (such as language or art) can be deducted as well as books, publications, trade and professional journals, uniforms, instruments, and tools.

If you pay your own medical insurance, you can deduct half the cost of the premiums up to $150 even if you have no other medical expenses. The balance can be included with other medical expenses. If the doctor prescribes or recommends a mattress, air conditioner, or humidifier, get his statement in writing and deduct. (If a permanent addition to your home is made, central air conditioning, for example, only the cost of the prescribed equipment which exceeds the increased value of your home may be deducted.) If you must take a trip to a warm climate to relieve a specific ailment, the travel is deductible, but not meals or lodging. If a parent must travel with a sick child, he can deduct the cost of his travel as well as costs of the patient's travel for doctor visits.

The dollars you keep after taxes are tax-free. The more you can legally keep on your side of the ledger, the more you will have to spend or invest. If math is not your strong point, find a good tax adviser, accountant, or attorney ("good" meaning legal). He'll show you how to keep your barters honest and may even let you pay your bill with barter.

And if despite the fact that your information and records are accurate and your intentions honorable the IRS decides to audit, before your feathers get ruffled, try hissing. It may make all the difference.

"Human felicity is produced not so much by great pieces of fortune that seldom happens . . . as by little advantages that occur every day."

—BENJAMIN FRANKLIN

Tools

Tooling Up

"Man is a tool-using animal. Nowhere do you find him without tools.
Without tools he is nothing. With tools he is all."

—Thomas Carlyle

A tool can be any instrument or machine—from a broom to a
tractor—used in the performance of an operation, or anything
necessary to carrying out one's occupation (words are the tools of
the writer's trade).

Some tool barterers are beginning collections while others are
adding to what they already have. Collectors may look for years for
a single tool to round out their collections. A craftsman or
shopowner may be trading up, increasing his capabilities for new
work, or retooling (removing the old to bring in the new).

Need for tools can be for private or public, for use as a home-
owner, a new second-home owner, a fledgling businessman, or
someone who absolutely cannot walk away from anything with
wheels. Before you start matching your needs with those of
another tool owner, decide which sort of tool barterer you are,
what you are willing to trade, and whether tool-collecting is a full-
or part-time avocation.

If you look around you and watch for things that others miss, all
kinds of tools will come your way. Walk to where you are going instead of driving; use back alleys instead of sidewalks (no one
leaves old tools on the front steps). Many people don't want unnecessary tools and machines lying around but can't find someone
to haul them away (offer to do so). Recognize tools made into other
things (lamps or table bases); find a substitute and offer to trade (it

may be the best offer they've had all year). When you attend auctions at private residences, check outbuildings for odds and ends of tools not important enough to be included in the sale; then offer to help the auctioneer clean up in return for getting them. Or arrive early and help him set up in return for what you seek. Offer to take tools your friends don't want (if you have storage space), later trading them for what you prefer.

Whether you are looking for a single tool or indulging a full-time mania will determine how far you should go in time and effort. If it's the latter, sharing knowledge will get you on the inside track. Give free information to people who ask about the value or use of tools at an auction. The next time they hear of available tools, you'll be the first to be called. If you are comfortable to do business with, you may be the first one "pickers" call when they find unusual items. If they know you already have a particular tool, they may call because they don't know its worth and want a free appraisal. Calling this to their attention won't help—they will only stop asking and you will miss some bargains. Before long, you will be matching finds you don't want with those you do, and getting a free leg on future favors and barters.

If you find yourself with duplicates, trade them off for others at flea markets and community/farm auctions, or trade for repairs on those you want to keep. Set up a local tool exchange with your garage as home base (this will bring exciting new discoveries to your door, while saving time and gas). If you have a great number of tools, hold an auction; or trade them in at the local junkyard for other things. Organize an equipment auction in your region where farmers and businessmen bring unused equipment annually to trade or sell (giving you as manager first choice). If the sale outgrows your yard, barter for the use of the local fairgrounds, giving the board a percentage of sales in place of rent. This type of activity gives you access to additional multi-barters or parlays, which can be arranged on paper with each new owner picking up his tool from the previous location.

Turn somebody else's problem into your asset. Help a friend clean out his garage and offer to take "unnecessary" tools off his hands. Go into the garage- and basement-cleaning business on the condition you get first tabs on unwanteds (or better yet, talk your

children into going into the garage-cleaning business and get first
tabs on what they bring home; they'll be earning money and you'll
be gaining tools). Either way, you will be dealing with quantity
which will, in turn, increase sources and outlets.

Shop the dump. *Landfill* is the contemporary word for a dump.
New users have a tendency to unload their cars or trucks of what
they brought to dump and then start scavenging what others have
unloaded, filling up their cars and taking home more than they
brought in the first place.

Perhaps you covet a windmill? Find one unused, knock on the
farmer's door, and ask what he'll trade for it in services or goods.
Farmers are old hands at barter and often prefer exchange to
money. If the barter succeeds, he may take you out to his barn for
show-and-tell (and more goodies).

Barter by sharing what you have. This may or may not be tools; it
could be experience. Being able to show someone else how to use
his tools (whether a hand plow or a farmhorse) may give you free
use of it. If you don't have a skill or talent in repairing or using
tools, barter for a course in repairs or welding and become the local
toolman's friend. Repair tools for others on a regular basis; then
use what they own that you need. As an accomplished tool repairman, swap your services to a local tool rental outlet for credit on
other tool use, or repair a number in return for permanent ownership or a percentage of repairs. Tools that have to be mended
frequently usually are on their way out of use, open to trade, or old
enough to become antiques. If you know who needs them and set
up the barter as middleman, you may get a tool as commission.
Talents can be related or unrelated. Perhaps the person who owns
the tool you want would prefer help with the harvest, or if you are
a lawyer, legal consultation. Or he may want to trade your services
to the owner of what he wants to acquire.

Use of your tools or talents can be traded for other things (sharpening ice skates for a local sports shop or skating rink in return
for credit or free admission). If you are the new owner of an old
farm, swap tools you don't want to obtain services you need,
whether landscaping around the house or repairs for the barn. If
you have excess land and want to use tools but not necessarily
own them, work out a deal with a neighbor, letting him plant one-

third of your fields in return for use of his equipment (see Farming).

Barter free storage for use of tools or equipment, or work space where someone else can use his. Talk neighbors into joint ownership of mutually owned equipment; then offer your storage facilities in return for free use. If you live in a new development, instead of each person buying a mower, rototiller, or leaf rake, pool your money and buy them as a cooperative. Often if one person provides the storage or repairs, he pays in service rather than in money.

Work out a permanent deal with a repair shopowner that you will take all leftovers off his hands, freeing his space and giving you a source of free parts to use on other tools; or marry parts to get a whole to keep or barter for something else. You could even invent something new out of them and trade it for something special.

The rarest tools are usually obtained only through barter or trade; therefore it helps to become an expert. This may be easier than you think. Take courses, attend seminars, read books on tools, then when others need advice you will be the first they turn to, giving you first choice of what they find. If they decide their "unknown" is not what they want (and you want it), barter for it or accept it as a down payment on your accessibility as a permanent information source.

Craftsmen often trade tools with each other, but the standard rule is to return a borrowed tool in better condition than it was received, or as Henry David Thoreau advised, return Mr. Alcot's ax sharper than it was before it had been borrowed. Returning tools damaged or dirty makes you ineligible for another round. One of the first things an apprentice in metals does is to make his own set of tools. The second thing is usually to trade off his former tools (be ready!). The finest compliment a craftsman can receive is when the master who taught him gives him his personal tools on retirement. "Passing it on" in this case means not only the tools but the role of successor. If the master is tops in his field, the succession places the recipient in an enviable position.

Tools are extensions of human hands. Exchanging them is a handclasp of friendship, a sharing of experience, of work, the good times and the bad; like friends, the best ones are the most worth caring for—and kept the longest. As Willa Cather wrote, "These coopers, big and little, these brooms and clouts and brushes, were tools; and with them one made not shoes or cabinet-work, but life itself. One made a climate within a climate; one made the days . . . the complexions, the special flavor, the special happiness of each day as it passed, one made life."

Transportation, Travel, and Moving

Cruising without Bruising

Transportation barters cover everything and anything from getting yourself around the world to moving the local library down the street. If you have ever car-pooled, taken a charter flight, or applied for a group discount, you have already taken the first step.

Do you want to do it yourself? To get someone else to do it? To divide the work and expenses with one or more people? Or do you have the time and expertise to organize travel for a group in return for going free? Are you willing to share expenses and work in return for use of someone else's conveyance? To trade services, goods, time, or a combination of all three for tickets and/or wheels? To pay part to save time and effort? Does it matter to you how long it takes to plan? Is your occupation such that you can earn along the way, or can you take as long as you like reaching your destination? Are you picky about where you stay? Have you a talent that can command a free ticket (lecturer, masseuse, swimming instructor)? Once you match your lust for travel with someone else's need, all the details will fall into place.

Bartering for travel is not new. Columbus received three ships from Queen Isabella in return for staking claims on all territory and bringing back any riches he found. After years of war she was looking for a way to increase her treasury, while Columbus needed someone to underwrite his experiment.

But before you start, work out all details. Make sure who pays the expenses; if the vehicle is sturdy; and if one-way, who pays passage back. When wagon trains headed west in early days of settlement, many wagon masters learned this lesson the hard way. If another wagon master had to stop and help, he could not meet his own deadlines and might be attacked by Indians. To ensure this didn't happen any more than necessary, those in charge formed their own "insurance" through tradition: if a wagon master had to ask for help from another wagon train, he had to forfeit his horse's bells.

To encourage public transportation and help fledgling companies, states often bartered rights of way and free taxes to railroads. The Baltimore and Ohio Railroad (now the Chessie System) was made tax exempt by the State of Maryland when it first started. Although incorporated towns along the tracks now tax their improvements, the City of Baltimore still observes the exemption and refrains from sending them a tax bill.

If you're not eligible for a tax deduction to defray costs, try dividing the work and find volunteers. When it came time for the Bettendorf, Iowa, Library to move to its new building, the town was shocked to get a moving estimate of $1,100 to move 65,000 books. Because the library staff preferred spending the money on books rather than moving fees, they asked their 18,393 subscribers to check out three or four books each. The trucker who gave them the estimate was so impressed by their ingenuity that he donated use of his semi-trailer on moving day to move the rest of the furniture, and enough volunteers showed up to do the work. Cost to the Bettendorf Library: nothing for the move. Gained: much goodwill in the community.

If time doesn't matter, you could follow the example of Rod Morris of Princeton, New Jersey, who worked his way around the world—by bike. Trading work for food and housing along the way, he spent 75 percent of his nights outdoors. But this can't be done on a two-week vacation; it took Rod two years.

Where and when you start depends on where you are, where you want to go, if you prefer being alone or in a group; also whether you want to finish off the barter terms before you leave, along the way, after you get back, or on an open-ended, permanent basis.

Check out newspaper and magazine ads under Help Wanted, Opportunities, Escapes, Employment, Sailing, Services, Personals, and Travel to see what is available. Many people are already looking for others to share travel and transportation, terms depending on what you are willing to trade. Listen to radio swap shows. If you don't find what you are looking for, write your own ad, decide where it will attract people with whom you identify, and place it.

Check out bulletin boards and newspapers in colleges, government agencies, private companies. Get your friends to post your advertisement in their school or office. Some publications, such as *Yankee* Magazine (Dublin, New Hampshire 03444), print free swaps each month. If you prefer privacy, list a box number instead of an address and telephone number, to make sure your barter doesn't get out of hand. Once you find what looks like a good deal, make sure terms mean the same to each of you (who pays for what? who is responsible for each part?); then get it in writing to avoid last-minute problems or cancellations. In some arrangements the rider and driver share expenses, or the rider pays for all gas in return for sharing the car, arranging the percentages to terms that are comfortable for both. If you live in an area where automobiles are manufactured, call the assembly plant to see if drivers are needed to take new cars to destinations.

Before you start planning your trip, make sure you have all the necessary information (a stamp can save a great deal of work). Where do you want to go? Write to the state Tourism or Economic Development Division, or the local Chamber of Commerce at your destination, and ask for all available information in print. If you're going on foot, find out if there is a visitor hospitality group that will give you lodging; if you are a member of a fraternal organization, see if it has a chapter there and write to it. Cyclists need to know where the nearest hostel is. If you are bringing your own accommodation in the form of a tent or camper, is free camping available in local parks or scout camps? Find out what free tours or activities are available in the vicinity and any recommended along the way (wineries, chocolate factories, quarries, and so on); then write direct for details (hours; whether children can go). If you plan your trip to coincide with a campout or festival, you may be able to arrange free housing and entertainment while in town. Once you have your itinerary, divide your journey into days to see where you will be each night, then write to those regions. If you prefer staying in hotels and motels, arrange your trip so that you can stay in small towns outside cities whose facilities may cost half as much; or if you prefer downtown, check out older hotels. If you don't want new shops, saunas, and swimming pools, why pay for them? Planning side trips while in town? Ask the room clerk whether others want to go along for the ride for a fee. Let the total of their fares pay your transportation and admissions. See if there are any National Parks along the way. Sometimes they have free camping facilities, living history programs, nature walks, and free entertainment (Shakespeare, symphony concerts, movies).

Renting a car? There is a time barter built into most contracts: the longer you rent, the less it costs and the more benefits are included. If you get enough people to share the time or space, it could end up costing you nothing. Those who work for a large company or organization may be eligible for discounts up to 20 percent, obtainable even when you are not on business. You will have to show your company or organization ID and pay cash in advance, but you will be entitled to the full discount. Discounts are gauged on the volume of business a firm does annually. (If your company doesn't already receive one, suggest that it be checked into.) Car-leasing companies also publish restaurant brochures, placed in their cars and on counters to guide customers to local restaurants, which in turn donate about thirty meals for the privilege. The meal credits are then given to customers as promotion, or traded to radio stations for free ad time.

If you prefer going by air, did you know you can buy a tourist ticket and go first class if the tourist section is full when you come on board? (Stand last in line.) On English airways, if there is room in first class and tourist is filled, pregnant women automatically go first class while paying tourist rates.

Have you a friend who works for an airline? Ask him to get information on how the VIP rooms function. Find out what is necessary for admission, if there are free drinks and/or refreshments, and last but not least, if he can arrange for you to enjoy them.

CAB Public Service Section (1825 Connecticut Ave. N.W., Washington, D.C. 20428) puts out a "Consumer Fact Sheet on Air Fares" (discounts, how you can save money by flying at different times, and other tips). The Civil Aeronautics Board, Federal Aviation Administration, Department of Transportation (800 Independence Ave. S.W., Washington, D.C. 20591), will fill you in on current government regulations for group eligibility for chartering a plane.

Several European airlines will trade free rides in return for writing articles for their inflight magazines. Others trade airline ticket credits for writing brochures or taking photographs.

Although it is estimated that 90 percent of airline ticket barter goes unreported, there are federal regulations governing and (in most cases) forbidding it. Airline employees are entitled to free or reduced fare passes and don't have to declare the value as income. But all other air barters are tricky as far as taxes are concerned. If you don't believe us, ask Richard Nixon—the IRS made him pay the air fare on Air Force 1 for his children's trips. Airlines can carry consultants free, so lawyers and professionals sometimes come under this classification. However, the Civil Aeronautics Board must give special permission for all other free fares. Most free trips go to qualified accredited travel agents, but they must be employed full-time and have been an agent for over a year (these are called Domestic Familiarization Tours). Major airlines can give tickets only to their own employees, directors, parents, and immediate families, plus witnesses and attorneys going to court cases where people have been killed or injured. To save time and frustration, barter with international airlines. They are not hampered by as many rules as are the domestics.

Prefer going by boat? What can you do that's barterable? Are you a doctor, masseuse, hairdresser? Trade your services for a free cruise with pay, or take along another person (your spouse?) instead of accepting the money. Oscar Fitzgerald, a naval historian, gave three lectures on antiques each way in return for a free two-week cruise on the *Queen Elizabeth II,* including two days in Europe. Carol Cutler gave cooking classes. If you can play the piano in the ship's lounge for two hours a day, you may also be eligible for a free trip. Write or call various steamship lines and get your own answers.

If you discover you need experience as a lecturer to trade for travel privileges, write to the International Platform Association (2564 Berkshire Road, Cleveland Heights, Ohio 44106). This group holds annual previews for professional lecturers, actors, musicians, writers, politicians, and entertainers who want to join the lecture circuit. Members will criticize your performance, help you polish your act, and find engagements. If, as an expert in a field, you are asked to give a lecture in another city, you are usually offered free travel and accommodations. Where this also includes an honorarium, ask if you can exchange it for a ticket for your spouse. Chances are the answer will be yes.

Or barter your muscle and exercise. American Youth Hotels (National Campus, Delaplane, Virginia 22025) provides inexpensive educational and recreational outdoor travel opportunities on bike or foot along the scenic trails and byways of America. They also have 130 overnight locations and sponsor ski and canoe trips as well as foreign travel.

If that's too strenuous, write People-to-People International (2401 Grand Ave., Kansas City, Missouri 64108), an organization of private citizens who voluntarily communicate with people in foreign countries through letters, travel abroad, campus and classroom projects, and community activities.

If you are between sixteen and eighteen years of age, soon will be, or know someone who is, contact The American Field Service (313 East 43rd St., New York, New York 10017), an established international program organized to promote understanding through secondary school student exchanges in eighty foreign lands during the school year and summer programs in sixty countries.

Check the tourist bureau of the country you want to visit and see what is available in return for your services (lecturing, writing, and so forth).

If you own a radio station, you can trade advertising time for all kinds of freebies in travel (see Business of Barter and Media for other trade-offs, due-bills, and so on). Is a neighbor going on an extended trip or sabbatical? Offer to manage his house or apartment while he is away in return for a free visit to his destination. Carol Ridker's neighbor, who was going to Sri Lanka for two years, had planned on paying a realtor $2,400 for managing his apartment rental in his absence. They worked out a trade: the neighbor received personalized management service, and Carol got a trip around the world—going out via Europe and returning by way of Asia.

If your plans are not that grandiose but you want to go *anywhere* just to get away from home, check the local high school and volunteer as chaperone for their next class, band, or drama trip. High schoolers go to interesting places these days—backstage at Broadway plays to meet the actors, Bermuda on Easter vacation, or Florida during the winter.

Religious and fraternal organizations also organize trips, sometimes only to conventions but other times around the world. Many groups need help with planning and touring as well. If you are well traveled or a teaching professional who communicates easily, you may qualify as tour organizer and guide and get your expenses free. Some private charter companies will give you free tickets in return for getting together a group of twelve people, but most will not trade unless you can produce fifteen to twenty-five. One Yale student, who went on to become a millionaire, could not work regular hours because he was on the rugby team and in choral groups, so he worked his way through college organizing and booking Bermuda trips. If you are an art teacher, you can take a tour of the world's museums and charge it on your income tax as an educational expense (see Taxes). Or organize a museum tour, be the coordinator and guide, and make a profit. What else can you do to pay your way? If you are an antique expert, you may be eligible to guide special antique tours for dealers, antique publications, and organizations. If they already have a resident expert, see if he needs help and offer to pay half your own freight.

If you like to sail, call yacht clubs near you (see Sports and Equipment). Talk to the manager; check the bulletin board or newsletter for information on who needs a crew. If you don't find anything, post your own inquiry. If you are experienced, it may give you the edge over someone who isn't, but sometimes all that's needed is a body, male or female, to help with the work. (Your chances are improved if you can do something extra.) When you become really good, you may receive money too. John Weymouth works full-time but still goes sailing thirty weekends a year this way, spending as much as five weeks at regattas. He started by posting his name and telephone number at yacht clubs. You can do the same. It also helps to list your weight, because sometimes the only criterion in getting the job is how much you weigh.

If you have a family and want to take them along and can spend the summer getting to where you are going and back, try education combined with work. Follow the crops, aid with planting, harvesting, repairing equipment. If you have a truck or van it helps, but if you chart your route visiting friends, you may not need one. It will teach your children more about the United States than they can learn in history books and put that pioneer feeling back into your marriage. If you don't have a truck or van but know someone who does, find out what he would take in temporary trade. It may be help with repairing his house, being companion to his elderly mother, or mending his fence. If you are already known, you may be able to get a magazine to underwrite the expedition in return for an article on the subject.

A craftsman who enters fairs can plan travel to and from, deducting it from taxes (because you'll be making business contacts). If you know several other craftsmen who want to attend a fair on the other side of the continent, form a caravan, sharing tasks and gaining publicity. Convince a moving company that if it transports your wares free, it would make a great advertisement (the headline could be: "If you think moving one family is difficult, how would you like to satisfy thirty fussy craftsmen?"). Or if you have an even greater number, find a sponsor and charter a jumbo jet. Barter deals like this are not as difficult to arrange as you might think. Meet the other person's needs and then get him to want to barter as much as you do.

Only need help with the moving? Remember the Bettendorf Library and rearrange your thinking and maybe your planning. If you have a truck, you may only have to barter for help. If you don't have a truck, trade with someone who does. One of us once borrowed a truck to haul bricks from a demolished house in return for contributing a painting to a hospital benefit. But she misunderstood the terms. When her friend said 8 by 10 she assumed the friend meant inches, but when the canvas arrived it was 8 by 10 *feet!* (It goes without saying who was the more experienced barterer.)

If you don't have to meet a deadline, figure out how you can move everything in smaller chunks with more people helping over a longer period of time. If you retain a moving company, visit them and see how you can barter away some of the cost—such as packing smaller things before they arrive, trading your services as clerk at disposal auctions, answering phones, or writing ads.

Moving a complete house including the walls may be more difficult. You could explore the house mover's needs and see what you have that meets them. If you own extra land, you could trade him land on which to build his own house. Or you could form a partnership with him and buy two houses, putting the second one on your land, selling it off, and splitting the profit.

Arranging a regular car pool is easier. Advertise where you live or work. If you don't get satisfactory results, try bulletin boards at educational institutions, radio swap shows, gas stations, and grocery stores. If that doesn't work and you are a super salesman who doesn't want to run up mileage on his car, talk a group into renting an air-conditioned bus complete with music, bar, and game tables. As the organizer and manager, you of course ride free. If your co-passengers don't agree, ask for a 50 percent discount. Better yet, form a corporation, rent the bus, contract the passengers, and make a profit.

Whether you are looking for transportation for yourself or an army, for a day or a year, across the street or around the world, there's always a way—through barter.

See also: Vacations.

Utilities: Heat, Plumbing, and Electricity

Alternatives to Life on the Front Burner, or How to Turn Down the Utility Company

Some years ago an irate Midwestern citizen, distressed by what he considered unfair charges, after getting no response from his utility company, declared war by installing his own generator. His neighbors thought it was a splendid idea and asked for hook-ups, at which point the electric company decided it was an absolutely rotten idea and sent out a representative to discuss his problems. They ended up buying his generator for a marvelous amount to stop the competition.

We're not necessarily recommending that you take such drastic measures in your search for alternatives to the high cost of (and sometimes lack of) utilities. There are many ways of bartering to offset utility costs, on a temporary or permanent basis. Some require labor, others joint effort; few call for drastic measures.

Have you ever thought of trading bills with the utility company? One time, when the telephone company parked a huge coil in a driveway without permission for three days, then drove it around the driveway hooked to a truck digging up the lawn with its tires and knocking branches off the trees, the owner of the property mailed them a bill for three days' parking, lawn repairs, and a surcharge to offset her irritation. It was paid. The next year, when the electric company sent men to work on high power lines going across the same property, the truck, instead of using the access granted by law, drove over the meadow, mowing down a rose hedge. When this carelessness was called to the company's attention, the truck made figure eights on the regular route. So the owner grabbed her Polaroid, took pictures of the tracks, and sent them with a bill for damages doubled by an equal amount for the insult, a total of $50. Again it was paid, and a public relations man was sent to assuage feelings and the repairmen to apologize personally. So don't feel helpless. Do something.

Windmills are making a comeback. NASA has a five-year wind-energy program to develop wind-driven energy systems to supply reliable energy at a cost comparable to alternative systems. It would take only 350,000 wind generators nationwide to equal the amount of electricity used in 1969, but if we can go to the moon, why not develop an up-to-date windmill? The windmills will be used to generate electricity directly, or the electric energy will be stored as hydrogen derived by electrolyzing water or as water in an elevated reservoir. Or energy extracted from the wind will be converted and stored as compressed air, then used to drive air turbines, which in turn would drive electric generators when needed. Wind-conversion systems with 200-foot-long propeller blades on towers as high as 1,000 feet are envisioned, or a large tower built to support many smaller rotor generator units. Windmills are currently used throughout the United States on farms to pump water and make electricity. If you live in a high rise, you are probably out of luck; but if you live in the country, you can save electricity in your system through partial use (such as pumping water to the barn). How to get one? Drive around the countryside, find one unused, knock on the door of the owner, and make an offer. If he is not using it and has no plans for future implementation, you may get it for less barter than you expect.

Or build a new windmill: barter your time and labor, sometimes a picture of the finished product, for a chance to construct at cost.

Mother Earth News has put out two reprints on wind-energy machines, each obtainable for 10¢ and a self-addressed stamped envelope (P.O. Box 70, Hendersonville, North Carolina 28739). Savonius rigs (once called Stuart Mills) are described in No. 183. Directions are obtainable from *Earthmind* (26510 Josel Dr., Saugus, California 91350) in a packet for $7.50. You'll get a refund of $3 on your order if you send a photo of the completed rotor-driven plant and a description of any modifications you have made, and a form to complete for *Earthmind*'s library (a worthy barter in itself). This nonprofit organization, formed for research and education, has a farm full of solar and wind-energy devices which it will show you if you're in the neighborhood. A Canadian-designed five-rotor pump which can be built for $51 is described in reprint No. 155. (Detailed plans are obtainable for only 75¢ by writing to Brace Research Institute, Macdonald College of McGill University, Ste. Anne de Bellevue 800, Quebec, Canada; ask for leaflet L-5, as well as a list of other publications regarding wind and solar energy projects.)

Coal is also staging a comeback as an alternative to wood for fireplaces because it burns more slowly. If you live in a coal region, seek out farmers who dig their own and will dig some for you in return for their needs (see Farming).

The gas company is considering a barter with the 34 million homeowners heating houses with gas. Michigan started hearings in March 1977 and at least ten other states are reviewing the offer. If it goes through, the gas company will offer to insulate your attic and install an automatic thermostat to improve your furnace efficiency—free (with costs passed on to customers in rate increases).

There are many ways to barter the high cost of oil. Check with your distributor. Some give discounts to groups or organizations, while others, organized as co-ops, return an annual rebate check for up to 15 percent of your bill. Others give discount for paying cash on delivery to save billing. It isn't given automatically; you have to ask. Other distributors will grant a finder's fee of $10 to $15 credit for each new customer you find. If you secure a large account, such as a hotel or college, you can get a credit of up to 5 percent of the first year's bill (5 percent of $20,000 is a healthy amount). If you are already a large account, ask your fuel man why you can't get fuel direct instead of going through a middle-man. But again, you have to ask. If you are engaged in an occupation such as real estate, selling many homes, you are in a position to pay your entire year's fuel bill by sending customers to your supplier.

If you are going to build a new house, check into what kind of discount a solar heat company will offer you in return for letting your house serve as an experimental model to promote sales in your area. In exchange for showing the installation to prospective buyers a scheduled number of hours or days a month, or even by appointment, you may get the installation at cost. If you live in an already built home in a development and are interested in solar heat retrofitting, you may be able to talk the company into the same arrangement, depending on the number of similar models around you, and if your house has the right exposure and sunlight. In domestic applications labor is the highest cost. An individual can save up to $2,500 by doing the labor himself. Once he learns and does one more installation for someone else, he will not only have paid for his own but made a profit as well.

Wood? Nothing tastes as good as food from a wood-burning stove, but sometimes the cost doesn't offset the pleasure. If you really want a furnace or stove that eats wood instead of the high-priced stuff, offer a one-to-one trade with the present owner in return for your gas or electric model. Wood, if you are willing to put in the time and work, is fairly easy to come by in barter. You can salvage it from roadsides, by cleaning up acreage, or after storms. You can make a deal with a farmer who owns woods to thin and clear his woods on a regular basis on either a one-quarter or one-half share arrangement (you get the larger amount). Highway department employees are often entitled to all the wood they can haul away after trees are cut down along the roadside. No need to go to work full-time—find someone already employed and barter for his excess. If he doesn't have it, he'll find it and probably deliver it to your house if the barter is right. You can also latch onto a great deal of wood by regularly checking disposal areas of companies dealing in electronic equipment, small machinery, or any product that requires protective crating. Make arrangements with them to pick it up on a regular basis, having them leave it in a separate pile until you get there. And don't let the lack of a chain saw slow you down. Barter with an owner to use his (for food, sewing, or use of your equipment); or if he doesn't trust it out of his sight, add on to the barter for his services. If your efforts produce excess, trade it off to anyone with a fireplace.

Craftsmen who find it hard to keep up with the cost of gas or electricity charges to fire their kilns can switch to wood or manure as fuel. To build a traditional Norwegian wood-burning kiln, one craftsman found an unused oil burner that once heated a chicken barn. The type of fire bricks used in its construction were exactly the type he needed, so he bartered firing Mrs. Farmer's pottery in return for the bricks; then arranged a barter for all the manure he wanted (in return for taking it away) so he could switch to dung firing (a primitive fuel that is never in short supply).

Someone's discards often can be converted to serve needs in ways you never thought of. Did you know that old refrigerators convert to meat and fish smokers? That stove burners can be converted to home kilns? And that washing machine motors do all kinds of things to boost the efficiency of equipment you already have?

When it comes to bartering for electrical repairs or renovations, you can't be too careful. The biggest problem results from selecting the person on a basis of need or personality. "It's a lot like love," said one dentist; "when you have your heart set on an arrangement, you can be taken advantage of. Stay nice, but keep your eyes open so you don't get hurt." He selected his electrician on the basis of his religion (definitely not the way to go). Although the man was a great churchgoer, his electrical work (done in return for dental surgery) was so incompetently done it had to be ripped out and replaced by another electrician, costing almost three times as much before it was finished. When hiring an electrician through barter, make sure he's doing it for a living. If he's not as capable as you think, his work could set fire to your house. If outdoor wiring is not done with the right materials, it will rust when water seeps in. Establish the cost in the first place, decide terms of the barter, and put the contract in writing. Ask for references. Set a deadline or agree on how many hours per day or week you expect him to work. If he doesn't get there until six months after the rest of the house is done, your furnace won't work and your pipes may have burst.

Plumbers are also easier to get through barter than you would suppose. Some will let you work as a helper to pay your bill. Others will see something they like in your basement while doing a repair and ask what you'll trade for it. If you settle for an open-ended barter, you may be able to say good-bye to plumbing bills forever.

Although some owners won't barter, the plumbers who work for them will if you approach them off hours and contact them at home rather than on the business phone. Retired plumbers on social security will do jobs for barter, as well as some whose unions allow them to work only a certain number of hours a week. If you see a plumber at auctions frequently, perhaps antiques are his weakness and can be a means to a barter (see Antiques). Some minor plumbing jobs like washer replacements can be done by novices; but to do a new house or move pipes, you need a permit, and you usually can't get a permit without a license. Make sure your plumber is qualified. If he's not, he could bleed your whole system and, if you live in the country, drain the well.

And if you're going to be away from home for at least thirty days, here's a way to barter with the telephone company to act as your secretary while you're gone. Call the business office and ask to have your service temporarily suspended (disconnected) for a service charge of $8, and give them a number anywhere in the United States to which you would like your calls referred. You can leave the number at your destination, an answering service, or the number of a friend who has offered to take messages for you. Then, when you return home, the phone company will reinstall without a service charge, billing you for only 50 percent of your monthly bill.

Down with utility costs! Up with life on the front burner!

Vacations

In 1955 Elsa Maxwell arranged the ideal barter vacation: a two-week Dutch treat cruise through the Greek islands with 100 of the world's greatest celebrities. Stavros Niarchos contributed the yacht *Archilleus,* as well as archeologist guides; a count donated 600 cases of champagne; American manufacturers sent gifts of clothes and chocolate to be distributed in ports of call; and the king and queen of Greece were waiting for the party at one of the stops. Elsa, in return for arranging the trip, went free.

Why did the others pay? Elsa found a need and, using her own style, matched the ingredients and came up with a winner. Greece needed tourists. Since tourists used boats, Niarchos benefited, so he chartered the yacht for two weeks in return for Elsa's guaranteeing the celebrities, whose presence would generate publicity, attracting more people. Elsa had the contacts. Once she invited the pacesetters and the newsmakers, everyone else on her list was flattered to be included. So much so, in fact, that she ended up with 120 instead of 100. Everyone paid his own way. Greek tourism increased 45 percent and has been on the rise ever since.

You say you don't even know that many *ordinary* people, but you still want to barter a vacation? Gardner Bradbury of Frederick, Maryland, used his hobby of woodcarving to earn a week's cruise on a 95-foot-long schooner. "It all started when I read that a sailboat would be launched in Maine," he says. "The article gave the owner's name and I wrote to him with the intention of carving the nameplate for the ship. He wrote back, and after exchanging correspondence, we agreed that I would do the carving in return for a week's cruise on the ship with my wife, son, and a friend of his." The owner was so pleased with the signs he now wants two more to attach to the sides of the hull, and Mr. Bradbury is planning his next vacation.

Where would you like to go on vacation? In search of the Loch Ness Monster? To a castle in Bavaria? Around the world? Alone or in a group? For a week or a year? It's yours for the asking through barter. Give yourself enough time to make arrangements and work out details. If you haven't made up your mind, stick with us and you'll soon be underway.

If you're a radio or TV owner (see Media) you can call your favorite media broker and arrange trips for yourself and as many of your clients as you like in return for advertising time. If you are a businessman whose company currently advertises on radio or TV, call your local station to see what's coming up in sales incentive programs or specials that you can work on in return for a trip. Maybe the station needs a space salesmen and your commission can pay your way. Full Circle Marketing Corporation (6500 Midnight Pass Rd., Penthouse Suite 504, Sarasota, Florida 33581) specializes in trading accounts with travel-oriented clients such as cruise ships, airlines, hotels, and car rental companies. Write for literature and see how you can fit your talents to its offerings and come up a winner.

If there's a special resort that you've always wanted to go to, write to the person in charge and see what you have in your talent bank that you can trade for accommodations. Older hotels might be interested in your setting up a two-week concentrated tennis clinic/workshop. Or, if you can lecture in a certain field, the hotel might build a seminar around you as a way of attracting other groups. Or maybe you could fill in while the desk clerk or secretary goes on vacation. Send for literature to see what bright idea will strike you. Then get in touch with the person in charge.

Or find the means that will take you where you want to go and make arrangements. Clare Walters, a New York writer, wrote brochures for an international airline in exchange for free trips. When pictures she had taken also interested them, she traded them for a free room at her destination, plus all meals.

Ken and Jackie Sola rented a cottage they own on the Potomac River for $175 a week to a family to stay for a month. At the end of their stay, the family asked if the Solas would accept their sailboat in exchange for the rent and were accepted. If you own a boat and want the house, but don't want to give up one to get the other, why not pick out a house at the resort you prefer that doesn't have a boat parked outside, find the owner, and trade use of the boat for use of the house on terms that suit you both?

There are many vacation home exchanges in operation throughout the United States. The largest is Vacation Exchange Club (350 Broadway, New York, New York 10013; 212-988-2576). Its 4,000-listing directory, mailed each January with a supplement in March, includes many homes in the United States, over 100 in Britain, several dozen in Europe, 50 in Canada, as well as some in the Caribbean, South America, and the Far East. You can receive a directory for $9, and a listing for $12, with an additional $5 for a photo of your home. The deadline for insertions is December 17, February 15 for the supplement. But once you make your decision, it's between you and the other owner. Adventures in Living (Box 278, Winnetka, Illinois 60093; 312-446-9522) issues a directory and three supplements. Insertions cost $20. Holiday Home Exchange (Box 555, Grants, New Mexico 87020; 505-287-3709) publishes every two months, with insertions costing $15. For those who prefer condominiums there is Concepts for Living International Club (499 Glen Street, Glens Falls, New York 12801). Others are Inquiline (Box 208, Katonah, New York 10536); Homex Directory, Ltd. (for British and Americans: Box 355, Pacific Palisades, California 90272), $13.50 for list and guide, $12.50 for guide alone. Once a house is listed, the rest is up to the matchmakers. Some exchanges have reduced rates for retired people, so if you are one, speak up. The Original Yankee Swoppers' column in *Yankee* Magazine (Dublin, New Hampshire 03444) publishes trades, either temporary or permanent, free, selected at random from ads of thirty-two words or less, sent in at least three months in advance.

Or, if you want to go to a specific area, write to the Chamber of Commerce there to see what's available. Or advertise in the local newspaper and see what offers you get. Maybe someone there wants to come to your place.

Even if your vacation is something that has never been done before, if you divide it into parts and work on one detail at a time, the pieces will fall into place. Or do something that everyone wants to do and get others to pay the fare. Have you ever wanted to take a houseboat down the Mississippi? You can rent one in Clinton, Iowa; LaCrosse, Wisconsin; or Winona, Minnesota, for $35 to $50 a day, depending on the size and season. Make arrangements before January to ensure the dates preferred, then talk two other couples into going along (or four people), getting a deposit to ensure their appearance. Split all costs between them, and you go free in return for making the arrangements.

Or try housesitting (see Housing for more details). Most sitters pay for their own food and travel, while the houseowners pay housing and utilities.

Change your pace and go on a windjammer cruise, on a safari to Africa, or hiking on the Appalachian Trail, trading your skills, labor, or knowledge in return for the trip. Find out where workshops are being conducted in your field and offer your services as lecturer free in return for registration and room. If you are a craftsman, check *Craft Horizons* Magazine (published by American Crafts Council, 44 West 53rd St., New York, New York 10019) for workshop vacations. Send your qualifications to the one you prefer to see if you can be one of the leaders. If your field of expertise is horses, check out dude ranches. A teacher? Plan the ideal trip for others in your field, then sell a teachers' association on the need to sponsor it with you as guide. (For more ideas, see Transportation, Travel, and Moving.)

If you own a second home or property but can visit it only a couple of weeks a year, convert it to income property, make it pay its own way and provide you with additional income to travel elsewhere. If you don't use it more than fourteen days a year, you can obtain the same tax benefits as if you rented it year round. If you show a net rental profit for three out of five years, you can claim all expenses, depreciation, and net rental loss. However, if you use it more than fourteen days a year, you can claim only interest, taxes, and casualty loss. Or, if you're tired of going to the same place all the time, trade yours for another by advertising in a newspaper where you would like to go, or in the Original Yankee Swoppers' column, *Yankee* Magazine (Dublin, New Hampshire 03444).

Use your vacation to do something you've always wanted to do, such as finding out where old mines are in your state, retracing battle campaigns during the Civil War, or unearthing treasure. That treasure may be your own genealogy. Starting with your family, find out everyone's vital statistics, where they were born and married, and places they lived, as well as names of relatives still living in those places. Spend your vacation checking out information, visiting courthouses, newspaper archives, and graveyards, retracing the past to pass on to the future. For a few stamps and letters of introduction, you can stay with newfound relatives and put some roots back in your life.

Or if that doesn't turn you on, and you are footloose and fancy free, find someone who travels a lot. Walk up and say, "I am your friend. I will follow you anywhere." See what develops.

Branching Out: Side Effects, Combinations, and Spinoffs

How you use barter depends on who you are, where and how you live, your age—and where you are heading. What motivates you? Power, affluence, influence, friends, material possessions, success, or a combination of all of the above? How much time and effort are you willing to spend to see your barters through?

Another factor to be taken into consideration, more often than you might believe, is the partner or spouse who isn't there, both on your side and on the other person's; or some unknown factor that restricts the moves of the play. Some people will barter for anything, anytime, anywhere, but others (for reasons known only to themselves) will barter only in specific areas (such as antiques or cars); or only in services but never materials. Trying to change someone's thinking on this score or even calling his attention to it usually does more harm than good. In all probability he recognizes the failing and can't or doesn't want to do anything about it. Forget him and start moving to where the action is.

Like potato chips, one barter leads to more. Everyone who barters knows more ways as well as additional players and sources. Once you start finding them, keep the game going. Don't slow down the action. The best barters are yet to come, preferably to you.

The possibilities, twists, and innovations inherent in trading are endless. Ploys, counterplays, interplays, innerplays, and side plays build up, depending on the number of players, the frequency with

which you play, and the opportunities you learn to see along the
way. The more you play, the more you learn. Specializing in a
subject or object (either informationally or materially) pays off because you have to put up less each time your expertise grows.
However, it can also have drawbacks in channeling effort or time
to specific areas while blocking out others. Stop and take stock
occasionally to make sure your barters are going in the same direction you are.

For instance, Phyllis, now restaurant critic for the *Washington
Post,* started by writing restaurant reviews for a small weekly
newspaper in exchange for meals. Since the job was in a neighbor-
ing city she lost money on gas, but she used her clips to sell articles to other publications, eventually working up to her present
job.

Connie, who has been writing for newspapers since the sixth
grade, wanted to spend more time writing books, but because she
had five teen-agers to support could not afford to—at first. After
bartering to restore and furnish her house, which was featured in
magazine articles as "The House That Barter Built," she started
bartering advertising and promotion talents and now heads her
own public relations firm. Barters don't spin off in only one direction; like mushrooms, they can pop up in unexpected new outgrowths. Since writing is Connie's main vocation, she must constantly keep spinoffs in their proper place so that they don't deter
her from her main goal: writing books.

Just as some people eat snails as an excuse for soaking up the
garlic butter that flavors them, some barters are only feints, with
their greatest benefits in the spinoffs. Shenandoah Outfitters rents
canoes in Virginia, keeping its river clean by trading the use of a
canoe for a bag or two of trash collected from the river. Nice barter. But what is even nicer, the project brings people to try their
canoeing and gets considerable publicity in local newspapers.

Don't consider each barter an end in itself; instead of watching
your feet, look where you are going. Bill Clark, who paints houses
to pay for his college education and to furnish his apartment, took
a broken air conditioner in part payment for a job. Next he found
an air conditioner repairman who needed a room painted.

Look where you are going literally, too, because many items that you may take for granted are sought after in other areas of the world. Tourists to Russia report trading ballpoint pens, gum, and button-down shirts for icons and medals. And anyone who has gone to camp knows how much more valuable his mother's homemade brownies are there than they are at home.

Look ahead when your neighbor is having a party now, and your daughter's wedding is planned for next summer. Or when your snow shovel fits the season but you don't have any hedge clippers to see you through the summer.

And once you get the hang of straight barters, try to execute some fancy steps. Take stock of your talents and barter them in combination rather than singly. Neil Shulman was a medical student who could write. Though just a beginner in both fields, the combination got him three book contracts in as many years, carrying him through his internship and residency. Along the same lines, a management expert who can score music has a powerful hand in dealing with a music company. Mike Curb, who started his own music company at nineteen years of age, sold it for $3 million when he was only twenty-two. At twenty-four, using his combined experience, he became president of MGM Records at $100,000 a year. At the time, the company was $17 million in the red. One of his conditions in accepting the job was the power to fire 200 or 300 employees. In addition to subtracting numbers, he increased his building power, strengthening and reinforcing his position; in only one year he put the company back in the black. However, without his knowledge and experience, he could not have demanded what he did; without the condition, he may not have been able to meet his goal.

To the veteran barterer, a crisis is another barter opportunity. A gas shortage starts a barterer arranging car pools, carrying passengers in exchange for whatever will save him the time he spends in the gas line. When a storm cuts off the electricity supply, a barterer gives a party, inviting friends to bring candles and pot luck. Besides sharing food and light, the guests contribute body heat to warm one another.

While a champion barterer is open to any kind of opportunity, it pays to develop a special area of expertise. If you learn about antiques, you can spot a good deal that others might not recognize as more than junk. An art background gives you the edge in trading with new artists. A cook can turn $1 worth of ingredients into an $8 quiche or an hour's worth of car repair.

Even better is trading your expertise, thereby increasing it. Teaching carpentry gives you a chance to perfect your technique and finish a project you might not have done. An artist's representative gets to meet the artists and dealers who will continue to be useful contacts. Once word of your expertise and willingness to trade gets around, barterers will come to you.

Keep your eyes open for ways to combine several kinds of skills into one profitable venture. An Annapolis psychiatrist, suspecting that some of his insomniac patients were simply trying to sleep in uncomfortable beds, combined his medical expertise with textile expertise to invent a kind of dry waterbed made of tiny beads inside silky elastic bags. A group of architects in Washington were finding it hard to get jobs, so they formed a group combining different architectural specialties and offered a day of free advice to the public—the best kind of advertising.

Collaboration, after all, has established legends in every field: Lewis and Clark; Rodgers and Hammerstein; Gilbert and Sullivan. Stapleton and Richman?

If you prefer straight one-to-one trading and want to become the local barter baron, find a natural location to make the job easier and to start people talking (which is, of course, free advertising). The town of Rockport, Massachusetts, had the right idea when they set up a swap shop in the town dump in 1971. Like a good compost heap, it made its presence felt, eventually winning nationwide publicity. A swap session in Canton, Texas, has been going on the first Monday of every month since before the Civil War (which means they must be doing something right).

Maybe you don't have a warehouse but think your garage would be a natural for a reciprocal trade outlet. Start where you are, build contacts in your spare time, and before you know it, you may soon have the corner on the local market. Or start a barter newsletter, charging for ads to pay for the free distribution. You'll be the first to know where the bargains are. Or find a new way of doing something and franchise it like McDonald's or Holiday Inns. If you do something better than anyone else, let the world know as soon as possible—*after* you have trademarked or copyrighted it.

Have you ever thought of making your vices pay their own way?

If you are a shopping nut and can't stay away from the stores, find others who can't be dragged there and shop for them on a percentage or hourly basis. Or form a wholesale club and buy direct from the factory, charging a percentage for passing on the savings. Setting up a money pool for purchases or collecting in advance will pay for your purchases. If you enjoy detective work, barter your ability to find things out. Product Search was a Virginia company that snooped out sources for anything from an herbal wreath to an antique baby carriage. All it took was a telephone and a mimeograph machine to prepare the flyers. Even easier are businesses such as Power Mouth, which would deliver any message by phone as long as it was not obscene or slanderous. Apparently there were enough shy people who felt uncomfortable with the telephone to give Power Mouth a flurry of business.

Find out what many people miss and specialize, providing it on a grand scale—hay rides or husking bees, for example. If the idea is original, newspaper publicity may come free.

For more ideas on what and where to barter, there is a magazine designed expressly for traders. Subscriptions to *The Great Exchange* are available for $12 a year (655 Madison Ave., New York, New York 10021). *Barter Communiqué* is a newspaper issued twice a year for $1 a copy, from Full Circle Marketing Corporation (6500 Midnight Pass Rd., Penthouse Suite 504, Sarasota, Florida 33581).

Often barters branch out into friendships—if they didn't start that way. The best barters, in fact, are merely extensions of friendships. Cookbook author Burt Wolf had an annual barter with a friend that lasted, at last count, for eleven years. Every year each friend chose anything the other had that he wanted. There wasn't much danger of losing a favored possession, because each could get it back next year. But it never worked out that way anyway. They took anything—a chair, a painting—but usually Wolf chose neckties, as many as twenty or thirty at a time.

Barters can also be unexpected. One of Lowell Thomas's fondest memories of his father, a physician who often took barter in payment of bills, was the time he treated actress Lillian Russell while she was playing at the Victor Opera House. Miss Russell was so pleased with the results that when she saw the doctor in the audience during a performance she threw him a rose, then left town without paying the bill. A *fait accompli* barter?

Learn to barter and you revive the nearly forgotten art of play. Bartering becomes a pleasure in itself, an enjoyable pastime. You look for excuses to continue the process. And your barter becomes the open-ended variety, going on forever with each partner trying to supply the other's needs and both trying to repay the other. Or you consider the world your game board and advance to the pass-it-on barter. You pass your child's outgrown clothes to your neighbor's offspring, and they do the same for somebody else. A neighbor brings you the wood from the tree he chopped down, and you have nothing he needs. But someday you have extra wood from your fallen tree, and it goes to another friend. The repayment is in oiling the wheels of society, raising by some small degree the pool of human warmth that comforts us all.

The End— or the Beginning

When you first begin to babble about barter, friends look at you twice and then say, "What?" You repeat yourself and they come back with something equally brilliant like, "You mean *b-a-r-t-e-r?*" spelling it out as if you didn't know how.

Ignoring their ignorance, you try it. You like it, and with practice, apprehension disappears, replaced by an exuberant self-confidence. You start talking to people you don't even know, making offers for things you see in their backyards (or, worse yet, under their porches or in their garages). Addiction sets in. It's hard to suppress a squeal of delight each time a barter puzzle falls into place.

You know you're hooked when money loses its sparkle. Prices

fall by the wayside as you start planning for needs on a job-for-job, quantity-quality-delivery basis. Whenever you do come into money (through no fault of your own) you find reasons not to use it (such as saving for your two-year-old's college education). For some strange reason, your wallet begins to develop an air of unfamiliarity.

Instead of sending bills each month, department stores write and ask, "Where have you been?" Magazines you once subscribed to (before discovering the barter trade-off system) send daily love letters, begging for a place in your mailbox at *any* price. Instead of pretending not to notice when you saunter into the bank to pick up your weekly supply of matches, the president invites you out to lunch, inquiring (now that your investments and savings have reached an all-time high) if you would consider being the new member of the board of directors.

Your daughter is bartering her way through college, and your son (previously known as the Dropout), after apprenticing his way to architectdom, has called to say that his latest house (made entirely of bartered parts) is the new centerfold in *Architectural Digest.*

Spring planting and summer weeding are but memories. Your annual food supply is now delivered to your door by neighbors sharecropping your backyard. Instead of scrounging pennies all year for a vacation that never did meet your expectations, your only problem is deciding between an island in the Caribbean, a flat in London, and a cruise to the Aegean. And, miracle of miracles, your depreciations, exchanges, and tax shelters have kept the tax man from your door for the past two years.

Dream? No, reality. Barter can do it. Transforming your vices into virtues while teaching you to specialize in your own God-given talents, it allows you to let go, freeing your thinking as well as your life-style. As your personal enrichment program shifts into high gear, overflowing into the lives of those around you, theirs comes back to touch your life in ways you never expect.

You become less dependent on checks, cash, and credit cards and discover (courtesy of barter) that the best things in life *are* free. You may never reach the point where you abandon cash com-

pletely (or even ask how to spell it), but you will find your own personal answers to the rising cost of living.

You will also discover that in every barter are the seeds of new
barters.

In our end we hope you will find your beginning.